Painting and Decorating
WOODEN SPOONS

QUARRY

© 2003 by frechverlag, GmbH, 70499 Stuttgart
TOPP 3198 Löffelkerlchen zum Verschenken
TOPP 3199 Löffelkerlchen aus der Küche
TOPP 3202 Löffelkerlchen zur Winterzeit
TOPP 3234 Löffelkerlchen für Kinderzimmer
TOPP 3235 Löffelkerlchen für den Frühling

First published in the United States of America in 2005 by
Quarry Books, a member of
Quayside Publishing Group
33 Commercial Street
Gloucester, Massachusetts 01930-5089
Telephone: (978) 282-9590
Fax: (978) 283-2742
www.rockpub.com

Library of Congress Cataloging-in-Publication Data

Painting and decorating woodens spoons : 115 step-by-step projects for making
people, animals, and fantasy characters from wooden spoons
        p.   cm.
ISBN: 1-59253-155-5 (pbk)
1. Painting—Technique. 2. Wooden spoons. 3. Decoration and ornament.
TT385.P375 2005
745.7'23—dc22   20402445
                                                                 CIP

ISBN 1-59253-155-5

Grateful acknowledgment is given to Monika Berger, whose work appears on pages 10–38; to Monika
Gänsler, whose work appears on pages 39–64 and pages 122–144; to Armin Täubner, whose work appears
on pages 65–92; and to Tamara Franke, whose work appears on pages 93–120.

10 9 8 7 6 5 4 3 2 1

Photography: frechverlag GmbH Stuttgart: Fotostudio Ullrich & Co., Renningen
Design: Laura Herrmann Design
Translator: Helgard Krause

Printed in Singapore

GLOUCESTER MASSACHUSETTS

QUARRY BOOKS

Painting and Decorating

WOODEN SPOONS

115 Step-by-Step Projects for Making People, Animals, and Fantasy Characters from Wooden Spoons

CONTENTS

Introduction

Wooden spoons have long been used around the kitchen for a variety of tasks. With a little creativity and imagination, however, you can easily turn what were once simple utensils into a collection of innovative and charming decorative figures, for both inside and outside the house.

With a little paint, poster board, and a few easy-to-find craft materials, you can turn any wooden spoon into a fun and eye-catching decoration. Invite friendly faces into your home. Herb and vegetable "spoon buddies" will make you smile in your kitchen, and pen holders and key racks can be useful in any room of your house. Start off the holiday season right by hanging up an Elk Advent Calendar, or decorate your garden in the spring with an Easter Bunny Thermometer. Let these projects inspire you to invent your own wooden spoon buddies, mix-and-match decorative ideas, or simply re-create the projects exactly. Whichever route you choose to explore, the possibilities for decorating wooden spoons are endless. Above all, we hope you have fun making them with your friends and family.

Basics, Materials, and Tools

Painting the Spoon

Apply a base coat of undiluted acrylic paint to the bowl of the spoon and about two-thirds of the handle. Place the unpainted part of the handle on a table underneath a heavy book and let the rest of the spoon extend past the table's edge. Alternatively, stick the handle in modeling clay or Styrofoam to hold the painted spoon upright. After the paint is dry, paint the rest of the handle.

Painting Details

Paint details with a fine brush. Use two coats of acrylic paint to achieve an even finish. Draw faces and patterns with fine, waterproof liner pens, acrylics, or puff paint. For very fine lines, apply acrylic paint with a fine brush or toothpick. Apply puff paint with a painting nozzle that has a 0.02" (0.5 mm) opening.

Transferring the Template

Place a sheet of tracing paper over the template and trace the contours with a soft graphite pencil. Turn over the tracing paper, pencil side down, and position on the spoon, poster board, or other craft material. Hold the tracing paper in place with masking tape if necessary. Trace the contours with a hard, sharp pencil to transfer the pencil graphite onto the object. (All drawings on the template sheet are reversed to accommodate this transfer technique.) If the base coat of paint is dark, use a light-colored pencil instead of the soft graphite pencil to make the lines easier to see.

(Continued on next page)

Basic Craft Kit

The following materials and tools are commonly used and are not listed with the individual projects:

- Nail scissors
- Silhouette scissors
- Pointed craft scissors
- Cutter and cutting mat
- Coping saw
- Hole punch
- Pointed round pliers
- Small, flat pliers
- Tweezers
- Piercing needle
- Sewing needle
- Drill and drill bits
- Hammer and small nails
- Clamp
- Fine sandpaper
- Glue pads
- Glue stick
- Wood glue
- Universal glue
- Hot glue gun
- Masking tape
- Foam pads
- Styrofoam sheets
- Tracing paper
- Thin cardboard
- Burnished binding wire
- Toothpicks
- Cotton swabs
- Hard and soft pencils
- Eraser
- Fine, waterproof, felt-tipped pens: black, red
- Lacquer pen: white
- Pencil: red
- Puff-paint pens
- Matte white acrylic paint
- Paintbrushes
- Water glass
- Painting rag
- Painting nozzle

To transfer faces onto wooden balls, trace the template as described above and cut the shape closely to size. Make several small incisions on the paper's edge so the paper is easier to wrap around the ball. Tape the template to the ball and trace the template lines with a hard pencil, starting with the contours of the face, then adding the details.

Assembling the Pieces

Assemble the components of most figures with hot glue. Stabilize the pieces to be attached with masking tape while the glue is cooling. Use foam pads between pieces to achieve a three-dimensional effect. Attach wooden pieces to the spoon or other utensils with wood glue. Strengthen and stabilize wooden skewers and sticks attached to the spoon's handle with small nails.

Erecting and Stabilizing the Project

Wooden spoons are often displayed upright on a tree stand. If necessary, widen the existing hole of the stand with a drill bit that matches the handle's diameter. (Use a clamp to keep the base in place while using a drill.) Insert the handle in the hole and set in position with wood glue or hot glue. Another method of displaying the projects is to attach the projects to walls or doors. Use double-sided adhesive pads, or glue or nail a frame hanger to the back of the spoon, and hang from the wall or a door.

Making Faces

Transfer the faces as described above and draw on the mouth and eyes with a fine-point waterproof pen. For the nose, attach with hot glue a painted wooden ball (with a hole drilled halfway through the ball), a halved cotton ball (cut in half with a cutter and a suitable cutting mat), or a pompom. Stick smaller pieces to the tip of a pencil or wooden skewer to make them easier to hold while painting. If necessary, use small, flat pliers or tweezers to transfer the pieces. Draw on the cheeks with a red pencil. Use a cutter to scrape some color from the pencil tip and rub it onto the face with your index finger. If you prefer to use acrylic paint, moisten a cotton swab with a tiny bit of paint and dab on the cheeks. (Tap the cotton swab onto a piece of paper or a painting rag to get rid of excess paint.) Use a white lacquer pen to create light reflections on the eyes and nose. Alternatively, use a needle or toothpick to dab on white acrylic paint.

Making Felt Pieces

As felt is relatively unstable, affix it to poster board before cutting it to size and gluing it on to the wooden spoon. The template contours are transferred the wrong way round (see Transferring the Template, page 7, but use the soft pencil first, and then turn over the paper and trace the lines again with a hard pencil). Cut out the piece and attach it with a hot glue gun. For some ears, a gluing edge may be indicated. If so, fold the felt backward on the dotted line and attach with the gluing surface onto the edge of the spoon bowl. Some figures wear scarves that are cut from felt and tied or glued around the neck. This is done easily using a little hot glue or wood glue beneath the scarf.

Making Wooden Pieces

To attach wooden ears or other features directly to the edge of the spoon's bowl, begin by making a template. Place the spoon on balsa wood and trace the bowl shape. (Balsa wood is available from any good craft store or shop that specializes in modeling supplies.) Determine the size of the ears or other features desired for the project. Cut the wood to size with a cutter or craft knife with a new blade and a cutting mat. Smooth the edges with fine sandpaper.

For larger components, you can use very firm, thick cardboard or plywood instead of balsa wood. Use a coping saw to cut the plywood (size 4 blades are easy to use and will not split the wood, even if the saw slips). Smooth the edges first with coarse sandpaper and finish with a finer grade.

Attach large wooden parts with wood glue and smaller components with hot glue.

Structural Snow Paint

Apply structural snow paint to large areas with a bristle brush. For hats, brush the snow onto the brim. Apply snow paint to smaller areas with a toothpick.

Spoon Buddies for All Occasions

Dear wooden spoon owners: admit it—how much attention have you recently paid to your wooden spoons? Don't worry, even living with an artist they had a rather sorry life in the kitchen drawer, coming out only to stir pasta and sauce. One evening I looked a little closer at a spoon.

The chiseled shape reminded me of a smiling face. A little later, I had created the first "spoon buddy"—the Lucky Pig.

The spoon buddy family grew rapidly in number and variety. I created useful and fun gift ideas for every occasion, including the Sweetie Kitten, the Cow with the Nametag, the Guardian Angel, the Whisk Flower, and many more.

All you need is some balsa wood or plywood, paper, acrylic paint, a few accessories, and a wooden spoon, of course. Take a look in your kitchen drawer right now! Have fun crafting, and enjoy giving the spoon buddies as gifts!

– Monika Berger
Contributing Author

Guardian Angel

Cut out the body, wings, and sign from plywood and paint as shown. Draw the face with waterproof pens. Tie a thick bunch of raffia in the middle and glue it around the face onto the edge of the spoon. Trim a few pieces to make the bangs and attach it to the bowl with a hot glue gun. Glue a few strands together to keep the raffia from sticking out, and cut the hair into shape.

Drill a hole into one of the small spoons and into the sign. Bend the wire into the desired shape around a pencil. Attach each wing to the back with a glue gun. Following the template, attach the spoons behind the body with wood glue and then add the wings. Attach a picture hanger to the bowl. Attach the flowerpot to the dress with hot glue.

Materials for Guardian Angel

- 1 wooden spoon, oval bowl, 14" (35 cm) long
- 4 wooden spoons, round bowl, about $1^{1}/_{2}$" x 8" (4 x 20 cm)
- 2 pieces of plywood, $^{1}/_{4}$" (4 mm) thick, $8^{1}/_{2}$" x 11" (approx. A4)
- Matte acrylic paint: orange, beige, red, yellow, grass-green
- 1 half-flowerpot, $2^{1}/_{2}$" x $2^{3}/_{4}$" (6 x 7 cm)
- Raffia: natural
- Fabric flower trim
- Frame hanger
- Template

Materials for Baby Bear Freddy

- 1 wooden spoon, round bowl, about 13" (33 cm)
- 2 concave untreated wooden disks, about 1" (2.5 cm) in diameter
- 1 tree stand, 2³/₄ " x 3¹/₂" (7 x 9 cm)
- 1 wooden picture frame, 5" x 6¹/₂" (12.5 x 17 cm)
- Matte acrylic paint: Indian yellow, orange
- Felt pieces: ochre, light brown
- Poster board pieces: ochre, light brown
- Template

Baby Bear Freddy

Use a coping saw to shorten the spoon handle to 10¹/₂" (26 cm) or to suit the size of the picture frame. Apply a yellow base coat of paint to the spoon, the wooden disks, and the tree stand. Paint the picture frame orange. Let dry. Draw the face with waterproof felt-tipped pens and a red pencil. Make the nose and ears from felt (with a poster board base) and attach the inner ear with wood glue. Glue the ears to the bottom spoon edge and attach the nose to the spoon bowl with a glue pad. Insert the spoon handle into the tree stand. (You may want to strengthen the point of contact with glue.) Glue the wooden disks as hands to the picture frame and place the frame on the stand.

Mar. 4 - arrival!

Aunt Carmen
Spoonville, NY
USA

Materials for Butterfly Wanda

- 1 wooden spoon, oval bowl, 9$\frac{1}{2}$" (24 cm) long
- Plywood, $\frac{1}{4}$" (4 mm) thick, 8$\frac{1}{2}$" x 11" (approx. A4)
- Matte acrylic paint: pink, light blue, light green, orange
- 1 miniature clothespin, 1" (2.5 cm) long
- 1 pierced untreated wooden half-bead, about $\frac{1}{2}$" (1.5 cm) in diameter
- 2 glass beads, about $\frac{1}{8}$" (3 mm) in diameter: blue
- 1 frame hanger
- Template

Elephant Mail Holder

Cut the ears, trunk, and cap out of balsa wood. Apply a light blue base coat of paint to the spoon, the wooden pearls, the trunk, and the figuring wire. Let dry. Paint the inner ears. With a waterproof pen, draw the face and finish the trunk. Dab on the cheeks with a red pencil. Paint the cap as shown, or as desired. With wood glue, attach the trunk and cap to the bowl and the ears to the back.

Use hot glue to fix the figuring wire in the hole of the wooden beads. (Cut the ends into a point if necessary.) Attach the wire about 2" (5 cm) below the head to the handle. Apply a base coat of paint to the board, let dry, and inscribe with a waterproof felt-tipped pen. Place the half-beads centrally on the board to make the feet. Attach the pierced half-bead to the end of the board. Fill the hole one-third with hot glue and insert the handle. Hold the handle in place until the glue is cool. Finish by applying a clear varnish to make the board scratchproof.

Materials for Elephant Mail Holder

- 1 wooden spoon, round bowl, about 2$\frac{1}{4}$" x 12$\frac{3}{4}$" (5.5 x 32 cm)
- 1 wooden board, cut to 8$\frac{1}{2}$" x 4" (22 x 10 cm)
- Balsa wood
- Matte acrylic paint: light blue, pink, emerald green, lemon yellow, black
- Figuring wire, $\frac{1}{4}$" (6 mm) gauge, 7" (18 cm)
- 2 pierced untreated wooden beads, about 1" (2.5 cm) in diameter
- 2 untreated wooden half-beads, about 1$\frac{1}{2}$" (4 cm) in diameter
- 1 pierced untreated wooden half-bead, about 1$\frac{1}{2}$" (4 cm) in diameter
- Matte spray varnish: clear
- Template

Butterfly Wanda

Cut the wings out of plywood and apply a base coat of pink paint. Paint the spoon, wooden bead, and clothespin orange. Let dry and then paint the hearts and dots on the wings. Paint on the stitches with a fine paintbrush. Draw the face with a waterproof felt-tipped pen and dab a little red acrylic on the cheeks with a cotton swab. Attach the wooden bead as the nose, paint stripes on the handle, and attach the clothespin at the bottom. Attach the wings at the back of the handle with wood glue. Bend the wire to make the antennae and attach at the back of the bowl. Then attach two small beads to the ends of the antennae. Attach a frame hanger to the back of the bowl; if necessary, use a small piece of plywood as underlay.

Tip

You can use strong cardboard instead of plywood to make the wings.

Ladybug Sweetie

Apply a black or red base coat of paint to the handle and paint the bowl beige. Let dry, then paint the face and attach the poster board nose with foam glue tape. To make the antennae, wind the wires, each 3" (8 cm) long, around a pencil and pull apart the coil slightly. Attach at the back of the bowl. Attach the wooden hearts to the ends of the wires.

To make the bug, decorate the handle with a heart pattern. Make the arms from chenille wire and attach painted wooden hands. If desired, attach a small present to the hands.

The ladybug's wings can be made from a painted wooden box, to be filled with truffles or other sweets. Paint the lid red and all other parts black. Let dry and then decorate with hearts. Attach the box to the back of the handle with wood or hot glue.

Materials for Ladybug Sweetie

- 1 wooden spoon, round bowl, about 2¹/₄" x 12³/₄" (5.5 x 32 cm)
- Matte acrylic paint: red, black, beige
- 2 small wooden hearts, about ³/₄" (2 cm) wide
- Poster board: red
- 1 heart-shaped balsa wood box, 4¹/₂" x 4³/₄" (11 cm x 12 cm)
- To make the bug, substitute black chenille wire, about 4³/₄" (12 cm) long, and 2 wooden hands, ³/₄" (1.8 cm) long
- Template

Whisk Flower with Teddy the Bee

Apply an orange base coat of paint to the whisk head and paint the handle and tree stand green. Cut the petals from poster board. Attach the large petals first with hot glue, then stagger the smaller petals underneath. Cut out the green leaves and glue them to the handle. Attach the handle to the tree stand. To make the bee, apply a yellow base coat of paint to the clay pot, let dry, then paint the brown stripes. Assemble the figure as described in the Template section. However, rather than cut the string for the legs, thread the string through the beads and finish with knots at each end. Cut the wings from iridescent foil, decorate them with glimmer paint, and let dry. Glue them to the back of the pot and finish by attaching the bee, centered on the flower.

Materials for Whisk Flower with Teddy the Bee
- 1 wooden whisk, about $2^1/4$" x $11^1/2$" (5.5 x 29 cm)
- 1 tree stand, $2^3/4$" x $3^1/2$" (7 x 9 cm)
- Poster board: white, light green
- Matte acrylic paint: grass-green, orange, yellow, brown
- 1 clay pot, about $1^1/2$" (3.5 cm)
- 5 pierced untreated wooden beads, about $1/2$" (1.3 cm) in diameter
- 1 pierced untreated wooden bead, about $1^1/4$" (3 cm) in diameter
- Iridescent foil
- Glimmer paint: transparent
- 1 piece of string, 8" (20 cm) long
- 1 piece of string, $13^3/4$" (35 cm) long
- Flower hair: red
- Template

Slowly the Snail

Paint the spoon's handle green and its bowl orange. Paint the yellow spiral with a fine paintbrush. Cut the poster board to size using the template and attach the pompom nose. Decorate the face and glue the head to the back of the bowl. Glue the bent wire antennae, each $2^3/4$" (7 cm) long, to the back of the head and attach the wooden beads to the ends with hot glue.

Materials for Slowly the Snail
- 1 wooden spoon, round bowl, about $1^3/4$" x 10" (4.5 x 25 cm)
- Matte acrylic paint: grass-green, orange, yellow
- Poster board: beige
- 1 pompom, about $1/4$" (7 mm) in diameter: red
- 2 wooden beads, about $1/4$" (7 mm) in diameter: orange
- Template

Fritz Welcomes You

Apply a base coat of thinned pink paint to the spoon and the wooden beads. Let dry and then paint the face. Attach the short pieces of raffia as hair with hot glue to the top of the bowl, and then attach the hat. Trim the raffia into the desired shape.

To make the shirt, attach light blue felt (cut to desired size and shape) to the poster board with a glue stick. Then attach thin strips of felt with wood glue to make the plaid pattern—any shapes will do. Repeat to make a second identical shape, front and back. Insert the arms, each 3" (8 cm) long, between the two pieces and hot-glue them together.

Attach the legs, each 4" (10 cm) long, to the inside of the shirt and then glue the hand and foot beads to the sisal string. (Cut the ends of the string into points if necessary for threading.) Make the sign from balsa wood, paint it white, let dry, and finish by inscribing it as desired.

Wind the wire around a pencil and thread small flowers onto it. Make the necessary holes at the bottom of the sign with a pin needle, thread the wire through, and attach the wire at the back. Glue the sign to the hands. From the bottom, pull the shirt over the handle and attach it at the back if necessary.

Materials for Fritz Welcomes You

- 1 wooden spoon, round bowl, about 2¼" x 12¾" (5.5 x 32 cm)
- Balsa wood
- Matte acrylic paint: beige
- Sisal string, about ¼" (4 mm) thick, 16" (40 cm) long
- 2 pierced untreated wooden beads, about ½" (1.2 cm) in diameter
- 2 pierced untreated wooden beads, about 1" (2.5 cm) in diameter
- Raffia: natural
- 1 straw hat, about 4" (10.5 cm) in diameter (outer rim)
- Felt: light blue, light green, lemon yellow
- Poster board: light blue
- 3 small textile flowers, about ½" to 1" (1–2.5 cm) in diameter
- Template

Materials for Bertha the Cow Name Plaque

- 1 wooden spoon, round bowl, about $2^{1}/_{4}$" x $12^{3}/_{4}$" (5.5 x 32 cm)
- 4 wooden spoons, round bowls, about $1^{1}/_{2}$" x 8" (4 x 20 cm)
- 1 wooden board, cut to $8^{3}/_{4}$" x 4" (22 cm x 10 cm)
- Balsa wood
- Matte acrylic paint: black, red, beige, white
- Sisal string, about $^{1}/_{4}$" (4 mm) thick, $6^{3}/_{4}$" (17 cm) long
- 1 fabric sunflower, about 1" (2.5 cm) in diameter
- Matte spray varnish: clear
- Template

Bertha the Cow Name Plaque

Cut the muzzle and the ears with horns from balsa wood. Apply a white base coat of paint to all parts except the muzzle. Let dry then paint the cowhide pattern and the hooves. Apply a beige base coat of paint to the muzzle and draw the mouth and nostrils with a waterproof felt-tipped pen. Dab on a little red paint with a cotton swab to make the rosy cheeks.

Attach the spoons with wood glue. Attach the muzzle to the bowl and the ears with the horns at the back of the head. Inscribe with a white lacquer pen and then varnish the whole plaque. Attach the sunflower to the muzzle with hot glue. To make the tail, fray one end of the sisal string and paint it black. Glue the other end to the back of the sign. Attach the wire hanger to the back of the sign as well.

Materials for Bride and Groom

- 2 raclette spatulas, 5$^{1}/_{4}$" (13.5 cm) long
- Strong cardboard, 11$^{3}/_{4}$" x 16$^{1}/_{2}$" (approx. A3)
- About 100 artificial ivy leaves
- 2 wooden beads, about $^{1}/_{2}$" (1.2 cm) in diameter
- Raffia: natural
- Felt, $^{1}/_{2}$" x 1" (1.5 x 2.5 cm): black
- String: white, black
- 1 top hat, about 2" (5 cm) in diameter (outer rim): black
- Polka-dot tulle, 2" x 10" (5 x 25 cm): white
- 4 miniature flowers such as forget-me-nots, about $^{1}/_{2}$" (1 cm) in diameter
- 15 wax beads, about $^{3}/_{16}$" to $^{1}/_{4}$" (5 to 7 mm) in diameter: white
- Balsa wood
- 5 wooden hearts, about 1" (2.5 cm) wide
- 1 frame hanger
- Thin wire: silver
- Template

Bride and Groom

Paint the faces on the two raclette spatulas and attach the wooden beads as noses with hot glue. Tie the two bunches of raffia at their middles, fix with hot glue, and cut the hair into the desired styles for each figure. Shorten a few raffia pieces to make bangs for the bride. Let the hot glue cool slightly and then attach the top hat to the groom. To make the bow tie, tie the felt in the middle with string, cinch, and attach with hot glue. To make the veil, tack the tulle, pull the string to gather the material, and sew into place. Glue the veil and the small flowers into place. Thread the wax beads onto thin wire and place around the neck as pearls. Tie the wire ends at the back and fix the necklace with hot glue. Cut out the cardboard heart to start the wreath and glue ivy leaves around the heart with hot glue. Make the sign out of balsa wood and inscribe the chosen message. Mark the placement of the holes and create them with a pin needle.

To make the dangling hearts, cut the silver wire to 1$^{1}/_{2}$" to 2$^{1}/_{2}$" (4 to 6 cm) long and attach one heart to each wire with hot glue. Thread the other ends through the holes in the sign and glue to the back. Cut the hanging wires (each about 4$^{1}/_{2}$" [12 cm] long), thread through the hole, and twist, using pliers if necessary. Attach the other ends to the back of the ivy heart and finish by attaching the bride and groom to the back as well. Attach a frame hanger at the top back of the ivy heart.

Lovebirds

Apply a white base coat of paint to the bowls, paint the handles green, and let dry. Decorate the beaks with yellow acrylic paint. Draw the eyes with a waterproof felt-tipped pen. Attach the feathers to the back and then glue the top hat to the groom. To make the veil for the bride, tack the tulle and fold in the seed beads. Secure the string and glue the veil to the bride. Fold the paper money into fans and push through the holes in the spoons to make the wings.

Just Married

Materials for Lovebirds

- 2 wooden spoons with tip and a central hole, 6$^{1}/_{4}$" (16 cm)
- Matte acrylic paint: yellow, grass-green
- 1 top hat, about 1$^{1}/_{4}$" (3 cm) in diameter (outer rim): black
- Polka-dot tulle, 1$^{3}/_{4}$" x 2$^{3}/_{4}$" (4.5 x 7 cm): white
- Thread: white
- 6 seed beads, about $^{1}/_{16}$" (2 mm) in diameter: red
- 2 marabou feathers: white
- 1 wooden heart, about 1" (2.5 cm) wide: red
- 2 pieces of paper money
- Template

Little Mo in a Balloon

Drill holes into the bowl of the spoon and paint as shown. Paint the tree stand green. Let dry. Inscribe a message of your choice on the painted balloon with a waterproof felt-tipped pen. Cut off the handle of the wicker basket. Use nail scissors to cut a 1/2" x 1/2" (1.5 x 1.5 cm) square from the bottom of the basket. Cover the wicker ends with hot glue to prevent splitting. Tie four pieces of string, evenly spaced, to the basket. Suspend the basket from the spoon. Thread the front strings through the holes in the bowl and glue at the back.

Attach the other pieces of string to the back of the bowl. Make sure that all pieces are roughly the same length. Fold the money into moneybags as shown, tie with string, and use double-sided adhesive pads to attach them to the basket. Attach the handle to the tree stand, using glue if necessary. Make the clay pot figures as shown in Template 2B. Tie the faux hair in the middle with string, cut to about 12" (30 cm) long. Lay the string double and thread it through the head and the inverted clay pot. Thread a wooden bead onto one piece of string, tie together with the other piece, and cut the ends to size. To make the arms, tie the string, cut to about 8" (20 cm) long, centered between the head and the body. Attach wooden beads to the ends and cut the string to length if necessary. Place the figure in the basket and secure with hot glue if necessary.

Materials for Little Mo in a Balloon

- 1 wooden spoon, oval bowl, 13 3/4 in. (35 cm) long
- 1 tree stand, 2 3/4" x 3 1/2" (7 x 9 cm)
- Matte acrylic paint: lilac, kelly green, light blue, lemon yellow
- 1 wicker basket, about 2 1/2" (6 cm) in diameter (outer rim)
- Thin packing string, 5' (1.5 m) long
- 1 clay pot, about 3/4" (2 cm) in diameter (at widest)
- 3 pierced untreated wooden beads, about 1/2" (1 cm) in diameter
- 1 pierced untreated wooden bead, about 1" (2.5 cm) in diameter
- Faux hair: red
- 2 pieces of paper money
- Template

22

Materials for Money the Frog

- 1 wooden spoon, round bowl, about 2¼" x 12¾" (5.5 x 32 cm)
- 2 concave wooden disks, about 1" (2.5 cm) in diameter
- Matte acrylic paint: grass-green
- Chenille wire, 6" (15 cm) long: light green
- 2 wooden hands, 1" (2.5 cm) long
- Poster board: white
- Sand
- Coins
- 1 plastic bag
- Ribbon, 1½" x 27½" (4 x 70 cm): orange-white-pink plaid
- Double-sided sticky tape
- Template

Money the Frog

Paint the spoon and the wooden hands grass-green and the wooden disks white. Paint the face and the irises on the disks and attach these to the bowl with wood glue. Attach the chenille wire to the back of the handle about 1" (2.5 cm) below the bowl with hot glue and then attach the wire ends to the hands. Use double-sided sticky tape to glue the coins into a plastic bag and then carefully fill the bag with sand. Hide additional coins in the bag if desired. Tie the bag with a decorative bow and glue on the greeting sign.

Don't spend it all in one place!

Hubert the Scarecrow

Cut the cotton craft ball in half and paint it beige. (One half is the nose.) Make the face, glue on the nose, and use a pencil to make it slightly red. To make the hair, use short raffia threads for the fringe and attach to each side two tied bunches of raffia, each about 2$^1/_2$" (6 cm) long. Put on the hat and cut the hair into shape. Shorten two crafting sticks by about 2" (5 cm) to make the arms. Place the even ends close together and attach the two full-length crafting sticks one after the other on top of them; this way, the shortened pieces remain attached to each other. Attach the felt to the poster board and then attach a felt mitten to each side. Decorate the arms, handle, and hat with small felt patches and paint the seams with a fine paintbrush or a toothpick.

Wrap chenille wire around the wrists to make the cuffs, attach, and then glue the arms to the back of the handle. To make the crow, apply a black base coat of paint to the clay pot and the wooden bead, let dry, and then hot glue together. Attach the wobbly eyes, the felt beak, and the feathers with hot glue. To make a hair tuft, insert a few small feathers into the bead hole. Attach the crow and the sign with hot glue.

Materials for Hubert the Scarecrow

- 1 wooden spoon, round bowl, about 2$^1/_4$" x 12$^3/_4$" (5.5 x 32 cm)
- Matte acrylic paint: beige
- Raffia: natural
- 1 cotton craft ball, about $^1/_2$" (1.5 cm) in diameter
- 1 straw hat, about 4" (10 cm) in diameter (outer rim)
- Felt: light green, sun yellow, red, orange
- Poster board: yellow, white
- 4 crafting sticks, $^3/_4$" x 6" (2 x 15 cm)
- 1 small textile sunflower, about 1" (2.5 cm) in diameter
- Chenille wire: light green
- 1 clay pot, about 1" (2.5 cm) in diameter
- 1 pierced untreated wooden bead, about 1" (2.5 cm) in diameter
- Matte acrylic paint: black
- 2 or 3 marabou feathers: black
- 2 wobbly eyes, about $^3/_{16}$" (4 mm) in diameter
- Template

Garden Gnome Edwin

Apply a beige base coat of paint to the bowl, the wooden bead, and the hands. Paint the top half of the handle (about 3$^1/_2$" [9 cm]) green and the bottom half black. Let dry and then draw the face with a waterproof felt-tipped pen and color the cheeks with a red pencil. Glue on the nose. To make the beard and hat, glue felt to a piece of poster board the same color and cut the pieces into shape. Glue the bird and the hat to the bowl. Attach the chenille wire, 7" (18 cm) long, with hot glue to the back of the handle, about $^3/_4$" (2 cm) below the bowl. Attach the wooden hands to the wire ends.

For the belt, attach a strip of black felt, $^1/_2$" x 2$^1/_2$" (1 x 6 cm), where the upper body meets the lower part. Attach the chenille buckle, about 1" (2.5 cm) square, on top. Attach the sign and the rake with hot glue.

Materials for Garden Gnome Edwin

- 1 wooden spoon, round bowl, about 2¼" x 12¾" (5.5 x 32 cm)
- Matte acrylic paint: beige, grass green, black
- Chenille wire: light green, yellow
- Felt: red, white, black
- Half-pierced untreated wooden bead, about ½" (1 cm) in diameter
- 1 miniature rake, 5¼" (13.5 cm) long
- 2 wooden hands, each 1" (2.5 cm) long
- Poster board: white, red
- Template

No crow can miss me!

the "sage" gnome

Cactus José

Paint the spoon, let dry, and then paint the face. Cut the nose from poster board and attach at the back of the bowl. To make the thorns, cut off both tips of eight toothpicks, dip the flat sides into hot glue, and use small pliers and tweezers to place them immediately on the cactus. Cover the label of the bottle with poster board. Cut out the general shape of the label in light green card, and then attach two other colored strips of card. Inscribe as desired. Finish by attaching the spoon to the bottle with hot glue.

Materials for Cactus José
- 1 wooden spoon, round bowl, about 1³/₄" x 11" (4.5 x 28 cm)
- Matte acrylic paint: grass-green
- Poster board: light green, red, white
- 8 toothpicks
- 1 bottle of tequila
- Template

Carlo the Tomato

Paint one third of the handle red, one third white, and one third green. Paint the bowl red. Let dry and then draw the face with waterproof felt-tipped pens, pink acrylic paint, and a green pencil. Use green poster board to cut out the nose and attach it with glue pads or hot glue. Decorate a gift basket with the tomato, or tie to a bottle of olive oil with a red ribbon.

Materials for Carlo the Tomato
- 1 wooden spoon, round bowl, about 1³/₄" x 11" (4.5 x 28 cm)
- Matte acrylic paint: red, grass-green, pink
- Pencil: green
- Poster board: light green
- Template

Günter the Fish

Apply a yellow base coat of paint to the spoon and the cotton craft ball. Let dry, then paint the face and glue on the nose. To make the cap, glue felt onto poster board, cut out the two template pieces, glue them together, and attach to the spoon. Use rainbow poster board for the bones and fins. Fold the bones along the dotted line (if necessary, use scissors to score the paper), and use hot glue to attach them around the handle. Glue the fin over the end of the handle. Inscribe as desired and glue onto a card.

Materials for Günter the Fish
- 1 wooden spoon, round bowl, about 1¹/₂" x 8" (4 x 20 cm)
- 1 cotton craft ball, about 1/2" (1.2 cm) in diameter
- Matte acrylic paint: lemon yellow
- Rainbow poster board: yellow-green
- Felt: white
- Poster board: white
- Template

Beware
of cat

for my little
mouse!

Kitty Candy Dish

Cut out the traffic sign, nose, hands, and ears from balsa wood. (Adapt the ear template according to the arc of the bowl.) Apply the base coats of paint as shown in the picture, including the backs. Let dry, paint on the face, glue on the nose, and use a brush to paint on the tabby fur. Draw the light reflections with a white lacquer pen. Paint the inner ears, add a red rim to the triangular sign, and let dry. Glue on the ears. Bend three short pieces of sticking wire into shape and glue to the bowl, using pointed pliers as needed. Draw the exclamation point and add writing and cat paw prints on the sign with a waterproof felt-tipped pen. Glue the hands and sign to the handle. Center the wooden half-ball on the plate and secure with wood glue. Fill the ball one-third full with hot glue. Place the handle into the hole and hold in place until the glue is cool. To avoid scratches, apply a clear matte varnish to the finished project.

Materials for Kitty

- 1 wooden spoon, round bowl, about 2¼" x 12¾" (5.5 x 32 cm)
- Balsa wood
- Matte acrylic paint: Indian yellow, orange, black, red, grass-green
- 1 wooden plate, about 8" (20 cm) in diameter
- 1 wooden pierced untreated half-ball, about 1.6" (4 cm) in diameter
- Matte spray varnish
- Template

Little Mouse Candy Bag

Apply a white coat of paint to the spoon and let dry. Transfer the candy pattern with a red pencil and fill in with a waterproof pen. (A graphite pencil would be visible through the red paint.) Cut out the mouse pieces and paint them light blue. Let dry and then paint on the inner ears and the face. To make the hair, bend sticking wire, about ½" (1.5 cm) long, into shape. Apply hot glue to the ends and push them into the wood with pliers or tweezers. Use a pin or needle to prepare the holes. Glue the mouse feet and head onto the bowls. Put the handle into the candy bag and tie with a decorative bow. Write a greeting on the sign.

Materials for Little Mouse

- 1 wooden spoon, round bowl, about 2¼" x 12¾" (5.5 x 32 cm)
- Balsa wood
- Matte acrylic paint: light blue, pink
- Poster board: white
- 1 small bag of candies
- Ribbon, 1½" x 27½" (4 x 70 cm): blue-white checked
- Template

Sylvia the Easter Hen

Cut out the wooden pieces from the balsa wood with a scalpel. For the narrow comb, cut out triangular peaks only and slightly round them with sandpaper. Apply a white base coat of paint to the head, the wings, and the bowl. Paint the beak yellow. Paint the handle, the clay pot, and the saucer green. Dab a little yellow paint onto the handle with the brush. Paint the small flowers on the clay pot with a cotton swab. For evenness and consistency, always add fresh paint to the swab. Fill in the comb and draw the eyes with waterproof pens.

Glue on the beak and wattle. Attach the wings behind the bowl with wood glue. Put the handle through the flower hole and glue it into position. Attach the chick to the flower and tie the eggs to the legs. Glue the pierced half-ball to the inside of the clay pot, over the hole. Invert the clay pot and attach the handle to the ball and the hole with hot glue. Center the ribbon beneath the saucer and glue. Place the clay pot on top and wrap the ribbon around it to tie it into place. Wrap the ribbon around the handle and tie a bow at the front.

Materials for Sylvia the Easter Hen

- 1 wooden spoon, round bowl, about 1³/₄" x 11" (4.5 x 28 cm)
- Matte acrylic paint: grass-green, sun yellow, red
- Balsa wood
- Felt: red
- 1 prefabricated sisal flower, about 2³/₄" (7 cm) in diameter: yellow
- 3 ceramic eggs with strings, about 1¹/₄" (3 cm) high: yellow, green, red
- 1 plush chick, 1¹/₂" (4 cm) high: yellow
- 1 wooden pierced untreated half-ball, about 1¹/₂" (4 cm) in diameter
- 1 clay pot, about 4¹/₄" (11 cm) in diameter
- 1 clay saucer, about 4¹/₄" (11 cm) in diameter
- Wired ribbon, 1¹/₂" x 31¹/₂" (4 x 80 cm): yellow
- Template

Materials for Easter Chick

- 1 wooden spoon, round bowl, about 2¹/₄" x 16" (5.5 x 40 cm)
- 1 two-piece papier-mâché egg, 5¹/₂" (14 cm) high
- Matte acrylic paint: sun yellow, orange
- 5 marabou feathers: yellow
- 2 sisal strings, about ¹/₄" (4 mm) thick, 2¹/₂" (6.5 cm): natural
- 2 wooden pierced untreated balls, about 1" (2.5 cm) in diameter
- Felt: orange
- Wired ribbon, 1¹/₂" x 29¹/₂" (4 x 75 cm): light green
- Template

Easter Chick

> **Tip**
>
> Hide some Easter surprises in these fun packages.

With nail scissors, cut out of the peak of each egg half a half moon – shape in the diameter of the spoon handle. Paint the papier-mâché egg white, let dry, and paint yellow over the white. Apply a yellow base coat of paint to the bowl, about one-third of the handle, and the sisal string. Paint the wooden beads orange. Let dry, then paint the details of the face. Cut out two felt beak shapes and attach to the face with wood glue or hot glue.

Attach feathers with hot glue at the side of the egg to make the wings; attach more feathers to the neck. With nail scissors, cut two holes into the bottom of the egg, evenly spaced from the spoon hole, and glue in the sisal strings as legs. Glue the wooden beads to the ends of the string. Glue on the wired ribbon, centered and secured around the chick's belly. Close the eggs around the handle and tie the ribbon in a bow at the front.

Easter Bunny

Cut out the ears, the sign, the chick's body, and the eggshell from balsa wood. Cut both cotton balls in half. Apply a brown base coat of paint to the spoon, ears, and both cotton craft ball halves. To make the nose, apply pink paint to the third cotton craft ball half. Paint the inner ears pink as well. Then paint the details of the face. Use hot glue to attach the nose and some raffia pieces as hair. Paint the sign yellow-green and the chick yellow. Paint the eggshell white and the beak orange, let dry, and then glue onto the chick. Inscribe the sign and paint the chick's eyes. To make the bunny's hands, glue on the brown cotton wool halves. Pierce the sign with a pin or a needle and attach the Easter eggs there.

Tip

For a more elaborate Easter decoration, use the rabbit to decorate a miniature wooden fence. To make the rabbit more stable, glue the handle into an untreated wooden half-ball. Cover the ball and the fence bottom with Irish moss and, if desired, place a small Easter basket and flowerpot in front of it.

Materials for Easter Bunny

- 1 wooden spoon, round bowl, about 2¼" x 12¾" (5.5 x 32 cm)
- Balsa wood
- Matte acrylic paint: light brown, beige, red, orange, yellow, light green
- 2 cotton craft balls, about ½" (1.5 cm) in diameter
- Raffia: natural
- 2 ceramic eggs with string, about 1¼" (3 cm) high: blue with orange dots
- Template

Get Well Soon Care Package

Cut the cotton craft ball in half and paint it and the spoon according to the photograph. Let dry. Paint the face and glue on the cotton nose. Add the light reflections with a lacquer pen. To make the leaves, glue felt onto green poster board and cut to size. Attach them to the brown chenille wire, 1¼" (3 cm) long, with hot glue, and then attach the wire to the back of the bowl's rim.

Cut the scarf to about 8¾" (22 cm) and drape around the neck as shown. Fix in position with wood glue or a tiny bit of hot glue. To make the orange's arms, center chenille wire, 12" (30 cm) long, on the handle and glue into position. To make the hands, roll up the wire ends three or four times. Glue the orange onto a juice bottle (which can be decorated with poster board). Attach the sign to the lemon and arrange with fresh lemons.

Materials for Get Well Soon Care Package

- 1 wooden spoon, round bowl, about 2¼" x 12¾" (5.5 x 32 cm), or with oval bowl, 10" (25 cm)
- Matte acrylic paint: orange, yellow, grass green
- Felt: orange or sun yellow, light green
- Chenille wire: brown or light green
- 1 cotton craft ball, about ½" (1.2 cm) in diameter
- Poster board: green, white, or orange
- Template

Santa Claus

Make the Santa Claus by following the instructions for Garden Gnome Edwin (page 24). Make the bobble for his hat from rolled-up chenille wire, about 3" (8 cm) long. To make the arms, paint the rounded craft stick red and shorten each end by 1/2" (1 cm) with a cutter or scissors. Center and glue the arms at the back of the handle and secure with a small nail. Anchor the arms further by gluing the cut-off ends of the craft stick over and below them. Attach the wooden hands to the wire ends and then use hot glue to attach the candleholders to the hands. Insert birthday candles and adjust the candleholders if necessary. Paint the tree stand white and let dry. Put the Santa Claus into the tree stand and decorate as described for Rudolph the Reindeer (page 35) with a felt bag and fir twigs.

Materials for Santa Claus

- 1 wooden spoon, round bowl, about 2¹/₄" x 12³/₄" (5.5 x 32 cm)
- 1 tree stand, 2³/₄" x 3¹/₂" (7 x 9 cm)
- Matte acrylic paint: beige, red, black
- 2 birthday candles, about ¹/₂" (1 cm) long
- Chenille wire: yellow, white
- Poster board: white, red
- Felt: red, white, dark brown, black, olive green
- 1 half-pierced untreated wooden ball, about ¹/₂" (1 cm) in diameter
- 2 wooden hands, 1" (2.5 cm) long
- Fir twigs
- Paper ribbon: red
- 1 rounded craft stick, about ¹/₄" x 8" (0.6 x 20 cm)
- 2 star-shaped candleholders, about 1³/₄" (4.5 cm) wide: gold
- Lacquer pen: silver
- Template

Materials for Rudolph the Reindeer

- 1 wooden spoon, round bowl, about 2¼" x 12¾" (5.5 x 32 cm)
- 1 tree stand, 2¾" x 3½" (7 x 9 cm)
- Matte acrylic paint: light brown, red, white, black
- Felt: light brown, light green, orange, light blue, black
- Poster board: black, light brown
- 1 cotton craft ball, about ½" (1.5 cm) wide
- Figuring wire, about ¼" x 8¾" (0.6 x 22 cm)
- 2 wooden hands, 1" (2.5 cm) long
- 1 metal bell, ¾" (2 cm) high: gold
- 2 small twigs
- Natural materials: pine cones, fir twigs
- Paper ribbon: red
- Chenille wire: white
- Lacquer pen: silver
- Template

Rudolph the Reindeer

For better proportions, cut about 1" (2.5 cm) from the spoon's handle with a coping saw. Paint the spoon and the figuring wire brown. Paint the hands black. Halve the cotton craft ball with a cutter and paint it red. Paint the tree stand white. Paint on the face and glue on the nose. To make the hair tufts and ears, attach the felt to color-coordinated poster board with a glue stick and cut out the pieces. Glue the tufts onto the bowl.

Fold the ears along the line where they will be glued and attach them to the rim of the bowl. Brush hot glue onto one end of each twig, about 2½" (6 cm) long, and attach to the rim of the bowl. Center and glue the figuring wire at the back of the handle, about 1½" (4 cm) below the bowl, and attach the wooden hands to the ends. (Cut the wire into pointy ends if necessary.) Cover the wrists with chenille wire. Onto one hand, glue the bell and, above that, a small bow. To make the scarf, cut the felt to 1¼" x 7" (3 x 18 cm), cut fringe into the ends, and glue on a small heart with wood glue. Drape the scarf around the neck and secure it with hot glue or wood glue.

Put the reindeer into the tree stand, securing with glue if necessary, and attach the hooves (felt glued onto poster board) at the front. Decorate the tree stand with natural materials and a small felt bag. To make the bag, cut felt to 3½" x 6¾" (9 x 17 cm), fold in half, and glue the edges together with wood glue. Attach patches at the front, and decorate the patches with seams using a silver lacquer pen. Tie the bag closed with a paper ribbon.

Pingu the Penguin and Snowy the Snowman

Apply a white base coat of paint to the raclette spatula and let dry; for the penguin, add the black coat of feathers. Paint the faces. To make the carrot nose for the snowman, cut the cotton wool carrot at an angle and glue it onto the face. To make the arms, glue sticking wire, 3" (8 cm) long, at the back of the spoon and add the cotton craft balls to the wire ends. To make the penguin wings and the two hats, glue the felt onto poster board, cut to size, and attach as shown. Decorate the penguin's hat with a chenille wire bobble and rim. Add fir twigs to the snowman's hat.

Materials for Pingu the Penguin and Snowy the Snowman

- 1 raclette spatula, 5¼" (13.5 cm) long
- Matte acrylic paint: white or black
- Felt: black or red, sun yellow
- Poster board: black or red
- *For the penguin:* Chenille wire: white
- *For the snowman:* 2 cotton craft balls, about ½" (1.5 cm) wide
- 1 cotton wool carrot, 2" (5 cm) long
- Fir twigs or similar natural objects
- Template

Tip

These figures make ideal gift tags. They also can be made into refrigerator magnets by attaching a magnet to the back with hot glue.

George the Chimneysweep

Paint the handle black. Cut the cotton craft ball in half with a cutter and paint both it and the bowl beige. Let dry and then detail the face. To make the hair, glue on some raffia strands, starting with the fringe and adding a tied bunch of raffia to each side. Add the clover to the top hat and attach the hat over the hair with hot glue. Let cool.

Drape the red neckerchief around the neck and glue into place. Center the chenille wire, 6" (15 cm) long, at the back of the handle, about 1¼" (3 cm) below the bowl. Attach the hands to the wire ends, attach the ladder to the handle, and place the left hand on the ladder. Attach the chimney brush to the other hand. (To make the chimney brush, wind the wire around a small round object and then glue a black wooden bead and a piece of chenille wire to the ends.)

Materials for George the Chimneysweep
- 1 wooden spoon, round bowl, about 2¼" x 12¾" (5.5 x 32 cm)
- 2 wooden hands, ½" (1.5 cm) wide
- Matte acrylic paint: beige, black
- 1 cotton craft ball, about ½" (1.5 cm) wide
- 1 pierced untreated wooden ball, about ⅜" (1 cm) in diameter
- 1 wooden ladder, 5¼" (13.5 cm) long
- 1 top hat, about 2¾" (7 cm) in diameter (outer rim): black
- Felt: red
- Chenille wire: black
- Raffia: natural
- 1 textile clover, about 1¼" (3 cm) wide: green
- Sticking wire, about 1/16" (1.5 mm) wide, 12" (30 cm) long
- Template

Louie the Lucky Pig

Apply a pink base coat of paint to the spoon, let dry, and then add the face. Glue the felt to the poster board and cut out the ears and snout. Fold over the ends to be glued onto the bowl rim and attach them and the snout to the bowl.

Cut the sign to size and paint it with watered-down white acrylic paint. Let dry and inscribe. Add the pink wooden disks and the clover. Attach the sign to the handle.

Materials for Louie the Lucky Pig

- 1 wooden spoon, round bowl, about 2$^{1}/_{4}$" x 12$^{3}/_{4}$" (5.5 x 32 cm)
- Matte acrylic paint: pink
- Felt: pink
- Poster board: pink
- Balsa wood
- 2 concave wooden disks, about $^{3}/_{4}$" (2 cm)
- 1 textile clover, about 1$^{1}/_{4}$" (3 cm)
- Template

Materials for Marcus the Lucky Mushroom

- 1 wooden spoon, round bowl, about 1$^{1}/_{2}$" x 8" (4 x 20 cm)
- Matte acrylic paint: beige, green
- Poster board: red, green
- 1 pompom, about $^{1}/_{4}$" (7 mm): red
- Template

Marcus the Lucky Mushroom

Paint the bowl beige and the handle green. Make the face as shown. Cut the mushroom hat from poster board and add the white dots with a white lacquer pen. Attach the hat to the spoon with foam tape. The mushroom can be given as a lucky charm for exams (together with energy-boosting food) and can also be decorated with a clover.

Spoon Buddies for the Kitchen

Are you looking for a completely different sort of decoration for your kitchen? Then look no further, as we have put together many fun ideas made from ordinary wooden spoons and other utensils. Create a chicken to help you keep rubber bands in one place, or a cat that looks after your oven mitts. Whichever idea you prefer, it will become an eye-catching addition to your kitchen. Have fun making these cheerful projects!

– Monika Gänsler
Contributing Author

Blackboard with Dog

Paint the spoon, along with the untreated wooden half-ball to be used as the nose. Make the ears, the mouth, and the paws from poster board and decorate with lines. Drill all the holes where marked on template. Draw the eyes and eyebrows and glue on the ears, the mouth, and the nose. Glue each paw to cotton wool cord, let dry, thread through the relevant hole, and secure with glue.

Glue the wire tail and attach the dog to the frame of the blackboard with a hot-glue gun. For the chalk holder, make a small spiral from binding wire that decreases in width at the bottom. Make a small hole in the wooden frame, push the upper wire end through, bend it over at the back, and attach with the hot glue gun. Tie the eraser and the kitchen towel to packing string and tie to the frame. Affix the blackboard with glue pads.

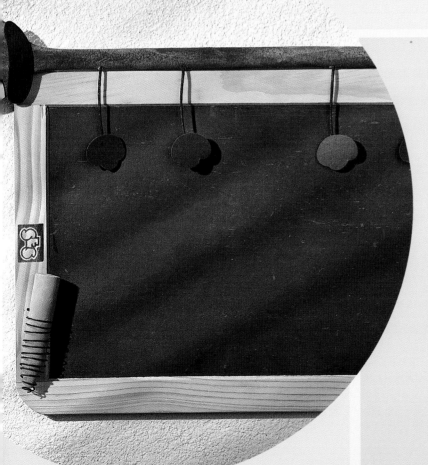

Materials for Blackboard with Dog

- 1 wooden spoon, long round bowl, 12³/₄" (32 cm) long
- Poster board: black, beige, dark brown
- Matte acrylic paint: scarlet, medium brown
- Cotton wool cord, ¹/₁₆" (1 mm) in diameter, 8" (20 cm) long: dark brown
- 1 untreated wooden bead, about ¹/₂" (1.5 cm) in diameter
- 1 blackboard, 7" x 10" (18 x 25 cm), framed
- Chalk
- Eraser
- 1 kitchen towel, 8" x 12" (20 x 30 cm)
- Packing string, about ¹/₁₆" (15 mm) in diameter
- Template

The Boss Is Cooking Here!

Paint the balsa wood sign slate blue, the spoon beige, and the wooden bead red. Let dry and then drill the holes; make those for the moustache from the front, those for the sign from the side. (The sign holes may also be made with a hole punch.) Draw all lines and redden the ears with a pencil.

Glue the assembled chef's hat, the ears, the nose, and the eyes to the spoon. Decorate the sign with two die-cut hearts. To make the mustache, thread a piece of binding wire through the two holes and bend them into shape. For the sign, thread the binding wire through the hole and then thread both ends through the sign holes and curl the ends. Drape a piece of kitchen towel, folded in half on the diagonal, around the neck, secure with a piece of wire, and curl the ends. Affix spoon to the kitchen door with glue pads.

Materials for The Boss Is Cooking Here!

- 1 wooden spoon, oval bowl, 10" (25 cm) long
- Balsa wood
- Poster board: white, red, beige
- Matte acrylic paint: beige, scarlet, antique blue
- 2 wobbly eyes, about $1/4$" (8 mm) in diameter
- 1 untreated wooden half-ball, about $1/2$" (15 mm) in diameter
- Heart die cuts
- Fabric (piece of kitchen towel), cut to $5^1/_2$" x $8^1/_2$" (14 x 21 cm)
- Template

Tip

You can use scissors to carefully cut the balsa wood pieces.

Materials for Cat

- 1 wooden spoon, round bowl, 12³/₄"
  (32 cm) long
- Poster board: charcoal, beige, black
- Matte acrylic paint: indigo blue, spring green
- 1 rounded wooden skewer about ¹/₈" (3 mm)
  in diameter, ¹/₄" (3 cm) long
- Cotton wool cord, about ¹/₁₆" (2 mm) in
  diameter, 4" (10 cm) long: black
- 1 wooden ball, about ¹/₂" (12 mm) in diameter,
  with hole about ¹/₈" (3 mm) wide
- Template

Cat

Drill the holes for the wooden skewer
where indicated on the template.
Glue into position and then paint the
spoon, the skewer, and the wooden
ball as shown in the picture. Let dry.
Make the holes for the whiskers from
the front and for the hair from the
side. Draw all lines and glue on the
poster board ears and nose. Thread
the cotton wool cord through the hole
and glue a paw to each end. Insert
one piece of wire into each whisker
hole, bend it over to the back, and
curl the other wire ends. Make a hair
curl and put it into the hole. Glue
the small wooden ball to the wooden
skewer.

Materials for Dog

- 1 wooden spoon, oval bowl, 12" (30 cm) long
- Poster board: beige, dark brown, black
- Matte acrylic paint: medium brown,
  indigo blue
- 1 rounded wooden skewer, ¹/₈" (3 mm) in
  diameter, ¹/₄" (3 cm) long
- Cotton wool cord, about ¹/₁₆" (0.2 mm) in
  diameter, 4" (10 cm) long: dark blue
- 1 wooden ball, about ¹/₂" (12 mm) in
  diameter, with about a ¹/₈" (3 mm)-wide hole
- Template

Dog

Drill the holes for the wooden skewer
where indicated on the template and
glue it into position. Paint as shown
in the picture. Make the side holes for
the arms and the curl. Draw all lines
and attach the ears, muzzle, and nose.
Thread the cotton wool cord through
the side hole. Glue paws to each end,
glue the wooden ball to the skewer,
and attach the curl.

Tip

Use a glue pad to attach
the oven glove holder to
the wall or cabinet. As the
prefabricated holes in wooden
balls are often slightly larger
than indicated, it is possible to
attach them after painting.

A Very Strong Chicken

Follow the piercing template to make the side holes, push the skewer through, and glue the wooden beads to each end. Then paint the chicken and the tree stand. Let dry and then draw the detail lines. Add the felt comb, beak, neck, and body. Put the handle into the tree stand, fix with glue, and then attach the feet to the handle at a height of about $1/2$" (1.5 cm).

Tip

Hang rubber bands from the arms of the chicken.

Materials for A Very Strong Chicken

- 1 wooden spoon with pointed tip, 12" (30 cm) long
- Felt: white, red, orange
- Matte acrylic paint: orange, scarlet, fir green
- 1 rounded wooden skewer, about $1/4$" (4 mm) in diameter, $5^1/4$" (13 cm) long
- 2 wooden balls, about $1/2$" (15 mm) in diameter, with about a $1/4$" (4 mm) wide hole
- 1 tree stand, $1/2$" x $2^1/2$" x $3^1/2$" (1.5 x 6.5 x 9 cm): natural finish
- Template

Lamb Rail

Drill the holes for the wooden skewer, insert the skewers into the holes, and glue them into position. Paint the spoon and the wooden balls as indicated in photo and let dry. Then drill remaining holes: arms from the front, legs from the side. Draw the face details on the poster board face. Color the cheeks and nose with a pencil. Glue on the ears and attach the hair. Thread white cotton wool cord from the back through the arm holes, add a wooden bead to each end arm, and secure with a single or double knot. To make the legs, thread a wooden bead onto each piece of cord, secure with a knot, and then thread the other cord ends through the leg holes. Glue a wooden ball to each skewer along the spoon handle. Drape a piece of fabric around the handle, tie securely with a piece of wire, and decorate with two small hearts.

Materials for Lamb Rail

- 1 wooden spoon, round bowl, 12³/₄" (32 cm) long
- Poster board: white, green, beige
- Matte acrylic paint: spring green, beige, black, olive green
- Cotton wool cord, about ¹/₁₆" (1 mm) in diameter, 6" (15 cm) long: white
- Cotton wool cord, about ¹/₁₆" (1 mm) in diameter, 6¹/₂" (16 cm): black
- 1 rounded wooden skewer, ³/₁₆" (3 mm) x 4³/₄" (12 cm)
- 8 wooden balls, about ¹/₂" (12 mm) in diameter, with about ³/₁₆" (3 mm) wide holes
- Heart-shaped die cut
- Fabric, 1" x 9¹/₂" (2.5 x 24 cm): checkered
- Template

Materials for Two Small Carrots

- 1 wooden spoon, round bowl, $12^3/_4$" (32 cm) long
- 1 wooden spoon, round bowl, 11" (28 cm) long
- Matte acrylic paint: orange, scarlet
- Raffia: light green, olive green
- Satin ribbon, $^3/_{16}$" x 10" (0.3 x 25 cm): light green
- Satin ribbon, $^1/_4$" x 12" (0.6 x 30 cm): green
- Template

Two Small Carrots

Paint both spoons as indicated in photo, let dry, and then drill the holes and draw all details. Thread raffia through the holes, and tie some wire around the base to secure the raffia. Curl the ends of the wire. Decorate the large carrot with a wide satin ribbon and the small carrot with a thinner one.

Onion Stick

Paint the wooden spoon as shown and let dry. Make the hair hole from the front and draw all lines. Thread raffia through the hole, wind thin binding wire around it, and curl the ends. Decorate the handle with a neckerchief.

Materials for Onion Stick

- 1 wooden spoon with pointed tip, 10" (25 cm) long
- Matte acrylic paint: beige, medium brown, scarlet
- Raffia: natural
- Fabric, 6^1/$_2$" x 6^1/$_2$" (16 x 16 cm), folded into a triangle
- Template

Moo the Cow

Paint the spoon white and the tree stand antique green. Let dry and then drill all the side holes. Paint the muzzle and sign as shown and slightly redden the ears and the nostrils with a pencil. Cut out the cheek dots with a hole punch and glue to the muzzle. Use a hot-glue gun to assemble the face and draw the eyebrows. Thread the cotton wool cord through the larger hole on the bottom of the handle and glue on the feet. Thread binding wire through the upper hole, thread from the back through the sign holes, and curl the wire ends. Put the finished cow into the tree stand hole and glue to secure. Glue the feet to the handle and tie the scarf around the neck.

Materials for Moo the Cow

- 1 wooden spoon, oval bowl, 12" (30 cm) long
- Poster board: white, black, beige, red, dark blue
- Matte acrylic paint: antique green
- Cotton wool cord, about $3/16$" x 8" (0.2 x 20 cm): black
- 2 wobbly eyes, about $1/4$" (8 mm) in diameter
- 1 tree stand, $1/2$" x $2^1/2$" x $3^1/2$" (1.5 x 6.5 x 9 cm): natural finish
- Fabric, 1" x $6^1/2$" (2.5 x 16 cm)
- Template

Fresh Eggs

Materials for Fresh Eggs

- 1 wooden spatula, 12" (30 cm) long
- Poster board: red, white, orange
- Matte acrylic paint: spring green
- Twigs

Fresh Eggs!

Glue the comb, beak, neck, wings, and feet to the chicken. Draw all lines. Paint the spatula, inscribe it, and attach the chick. Tie wire around some twigs, curl the wire ends, and glue to the spatula.

- 1 wooden spatula, 11" (29 cm)
- Balsa wood
- Poster board: red
- Matte acrylic paint: antique blue, olive green
- 1 rounded wooden skewer, about $^3/_{16}$" x $1^1/_4$" (0.3 x 3 cm)
- 1 wooden bead, about $^1/_2$" (12 mm) in diameter, with about a $^3/_{16}$" (3 mm)-wide hole
- Fabric, $6^1/_2$" x $6^1/_2$" (16 x 16 cm), folded into a triangle
- Template

Bon Appétit!

Paint the balsa wood hat and assemble the pieces as shown. Make the hole in the handle. Assemble the wooden skewer and wooden ball, insert them in the hole, glue in, and paint. Draw all lines. Add the nose, cheek spot, and hat. Tie a neckerchief around the neck.

Tip

This spoon will look particularly attractive if you drape a chili garlic necklace around it.

A Fiery Witch!

Make the side holes, push the wooden skewer through them, and glue it into position. Paint the spoon, the wooden balls, and the tree stand; let dry. Make the side hole for the hat wire. Draw all lines, attach the wooden beads as hands, redden the nose slightly with a pencil, and attach to the face. Attach the hair with a hot-glue gun. Fold a piece of binding wire in half, thread through the hole in the hat, and twist the two halves together for about 1" (2.5 cm). Thread a wooden bead onto each piece of wire and curl the ends. Drape a thin strip of fabric around the neck and secure it in position with thin binding wire. Put the finished witch into the tree stand and secure with hot glue. Tie wire around some twigs and attach at the bottom of the handle.

Materials for A Fiery Witch!

- 1 wooden spoon with pointed tip, 12" (30 cm) long
- Poster board: red, beige
- Matte acrylic paint: black, beige, antique blue, antique green
- 2 wooden beads, about $1/2$" (15 mm) in diameter, with about $1/4$" (4 mm) hole
- 1 rounded wooden skewer, about $1/4$" x $4^3/4$" (0.4 x 12 cm)
- 1 wooden bead, about $1/4$" (6 mm) in diameter: green
- 1 wooden bead, about $1/4$" (6 mm) in diameter: red
- Twigs
- 1 tree stand, $1/2$" x $2^1/2$" x $3^1/2$" (1.5 x 6.5 x 9 cm): natural finish
- Fabric, 1" x $6^1/2$" (2.5 x 16 cm)
- Template

Tip

Decorate the arms of the witch with chili peppers strung on thread.

Supplies Giraffe

Paint the wooden balls, skewers, and spoon. Let dry and then drill the side hole for the cotton wool cord. Glue the balls onto the skewers. Make the ears, muzzle, and cheeks from poster board and draw all lines. Redden the ears slightly and then glue them, the finished muzzle, and the horns with hot glue to the spoon.

Paint the eyebrows, attach the wobbly eyes, and tie the fabric scarf. Adhere the giraffe to the outside of the zinc container with a glue gun. Thread the cotton wool cord through the hole, coil it around the container, and tie in a knot. Thread a wooden bead onto each end and secure in place with another knot.

Materials for Supplies Giraffe

- 1 wooden spoon, round bowl, 12³/₄" (32 cm) long
- Poster board: beige, yellow, red
- Matte acrylic paint: black, medium yellow
- 2 wobbly eyes, about ¹/₄" (8 mm) in diameter
- 4 wooden beads, about ¹/₂" (15 mm) in diameter, with about ¹/₈" (4 mm) wide holes
- 1 rounded wooden skewer, about ¹/₈" x 2³/₈" (0.4 x 6 cm)
- Cotton wool thread, about ¹/₁₆" x 24" (0.2 x 60 cm): black
- Fabric, ¹/₈" x 8" (3 x 20 cm)
- 1 zinc container, about 4³/₄" x 8¹/₄" (12 x 21 cm)
- Template

Two Small Herb Sticks

Materials for Two Small Herb Sticks

- 2 wooden spoons with pointed tips, 10" (25 cm) long
- Poster board: olive green, beige, red
- Matte acrylic paint: spring green, scarlet
- Straw or packing string
- Template

Inscribe and decorate the signs. Paint the spoon as shown and let dry. For one of the spoons, drill the hole for the hair, thread straw string through the hole, and tie with wire. For the other spoon, tie a piece of straw string with a piece of wire, curl the wire ends, and glue to the head. Draw all lines, redden the nose slightly, and glue it to the face. Secure the finished signs to the spoon handles.

Materials for Goose with Toothpicks

- 1 wooden spoon, round bowl, 8" (20 cm) long
- Felt: white, orange
- Matte acrylic paint: fir green
- Cotton wool cord, about $1/16$" x $13^1/4$" (0.1 x 33 cm): white
- 2 wooden balls, about $1/2$" (12 mm) in diameter, with about $3/16$" (3 mm) wide hole
- 1 zinc bucket, about $2^1/4$" x $2^1/2$" (5.5 x 6 cm)
- 1 tree stand, $1/2$" x $2^1/2$" x $3^1/2$" (1.5 x 6.5 x 9 cm): natural finish
- Template

Goose with Toothpicks

Paint the tree stand and the wooden beads as shown and let dry. Drill the side holes into the handle and the head. Draw all lines. Glue on the felt beak and wings as well as the wire curl. Thread the cotton wool cord through the hole in the handle, loop it around the bucket, and make a knot. Thread a wooden bead onto each end and secure each with a knot. Put the goose into the hole of the tree stand and secure with a hot glue gun. Glue the felt feet to the handle. If necessary, secure the bucket to the handle with a glue gun. Finish by filling the bucket with toothpicks.

Small Lamb

Paint the spoon and tree stand and let dry. Drill the side holes and draw the lines. Redden the ears slightly and glue them, along with the hair, the cheek spots, and the wobbly eyes, to the face. Thread the cotton wool cord through the lower hole and glue on the feet. Thread binding wire through the lower hole, thread from the back through the sign holes, and curl the wire ends. Put the finished lamb into the tree stand and glue into position. Glue the feet to the handle and tie a scarf around the neck.

Materials for Small Lamb

- 1 wooden spoon, round bowl, 10" (25 cm) long
- Poster board: white, dark brown, beige, red, olive green
- Matte acrylic paint: beige, olive green
- Cotton wool cord, about $^{1}/_{16}$" x 7$^{1}/_{2}$" (0.2 x 19 cm): natural
- 2 wobbly eyes, about $^{1}/_{4}$" (6 mm) in diameter
- 1 tree stand, $^{1}/_{2}$" x 2$^{1}/_{2}$" x 3$^{1}/_{2}$" (1.5 x 6.5 x 9 cm): natural finish
- Fabric, $^{3}/_{4}$" x 6$^{1}/_{2}$" (2 x 16 cm)
- Template

Materials for A Sweet Little Bunny

- 1 wooden spoon, oval bowl, 12" (30 cm) long
- Poster board: dark brown, black
- Matte acrylic paint: medium brown, beige
- Raffia: light green
- Template

A Sweet Little Bunny

Paint the wooden spoon as shown, let dry, and then draw all lines and drill the holes. Attach the ears and the nose with a hot glue gun. To make the whiskers, thread one piece of thick binding wire through one hole on one side, fold it, and thread it through the other hole on the same side. Repeat for the other side. Curl all wire ends. Tie thin binding wire around raffia and glue to the handle.

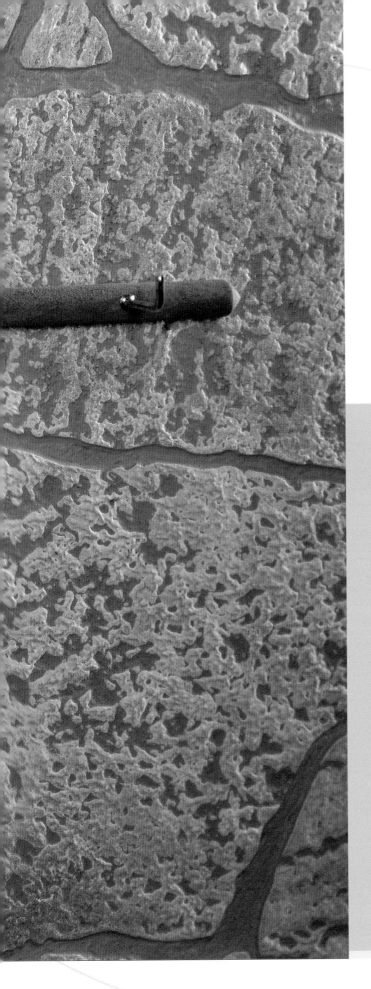

Piglet Key Rack

Paint the wooden spoon and the balsa wood pieces as shown and let dry. Draw the lines and drill the front holes (the holes do not have to pierce the spoon completely). Assemble the face. Make hair made from straw or packing string and attach. Screw in the hooks, attach the head with a hot glue gun, and add the binding wire and decorated button. Adhere the finished rail with glue pads where desired.

Materials for Piglet Key Rack

- 1 wooden spoon, oval bowl, 12" (30 cm) long
- Balsa wood
- Matte acrylic paint: raspberry red, light pink, olive green
- 3 straight brass screw hooks, $\frac{1}{8}$" x $\frac{1}{4}$" (2.6 x 30 mm)
- Button, about $\frac{1}{4}$" (11 mm) in diameter: pink
- Straw or packing string
- Fabric strips, $\frac{1}{4}$" x 8" (1 x 20 cm)
- Template

Materials for Don't Nibble!

- 2 wooden raclette spatulas, 5¹/₄" (13 cm) long
- Poster board: olive green, dark green, red
- Matte acrylic paint: scarlet
- 2 untreated wooden half-beads, about ¹/₂" (15 mm) in diameter
- Raffia: light green, olive green
- Heart-shaped die cut
- Template

Don't Nibble!

Paint the untreated wooden half-bead to make the nose, draw the lines, and inscribe the sign. Attach the nose and decorate the sign with small punched-out hearts. Adhere the sign to the spoon.

Two Salad Signs

Paint the untreated wooden half-beads to make the noses. Draw the lines. Inscribe the signs, make two holes with the hole punch, and decorate the sign with die-cut hearts. Drill two front holes into each spatula. Glue on the noses. Tie wire around the raffia hair, curl the ends of the wire, and attach hair to the head. Thread a piece of binding wire through the holes of the signs and curl the ends.

Materials for Two Salad Signs

- 1 wooden raclette spatula, $5^{1}/_{4}$" (13 cm) long
- Poster board: dark blue, red
- Matte acrylic paint: scarlet
- 1 untreated wooden half-bead, about $^{1}/_{2}$" (15 mm) in diameter
- Heart-shaped die cut
- Template

Tip

Attaching the signs with wire, and not glue, allows any number of signs you create to be used interchangeably.

Kitchen Guardian Angel

Paint the head and inscribe the wings. Paint a small dot on the shoulder of each assembled arm. Glue three thick wire curls to the back of the head. Paint the spoon as shown and let dry. Attach the wings, arms, and head with a hot-glue gun. Decorate a button with thin binding wire and attach it to one wing. Tie and decorate a small bundle of twigs with thick binding wire and attach it with a hot glue gun.

Materials for Kitchen Guardian Angel

- 1 wooden spoon, oval bowl, 12" (30 cm) long
- Poster board: beige, olive green, ivory
- Matte acrylic paint: antique green, antique blue
- Twigs
- Button, about $1/2$" (1.2 cm) in diameter: dark red
- Template

Winter Holiday Spoon Buddies

Ordinary wooden spoons are about to conquer the whole house from the kitchen. Especially in winter and around Christmas, they make an appearance everywhere: as Advent calendars for children, as place cards at a festive table, as a welcome sign on the door, and even as a thermometer on the balcony. You will see: with paint, paper, wire, and wool you will be able to create a diverse range of spoon buddies. If you still think that wooden spoons can be used only in the kitchen—think again!

Snowman Trio

Make the holes for the arms and paint the spoon white. Attach grass or abaca fiber as hair to the back of the hat. Secure the hat, paint the face, and glue on the nose. Thread the cotton wool string from the back through the holes and tie a white wooden pearl to each end. Glue the head to the body. Tie on the scarf, or glue on the bow tie, tied with wire, and affix the pearls as buttons. Add the structural snow paint. Attach the sign, raffia bows, and poster board heart and star with a piece of wire.

Materials for Snowman Trio

- 3 wooden spoons, round bowls, $2^1/_4$" x $12^1/_2$" (5.5 x 31 cm)
- Poster board: yellow, light brown, brown, green, dark green, red, white, gray, black, orange
- Felt: green, red, blue
- Abaca fiber: black
- Grass fiber: brown, yellow
- 3 cotton strings, about $1/_{16}$" x 10" (0.3 x 25 cm): white
- 6 wooden untreated pearls, about $1/_2$" (12 mm) in diameter
- 10 wooden pearls, about $1/_4$" (6 mm) in diameter: black
- Structural snow paint
- Raffia: natural
- Flower wire, about $1/_{16}$" (0.35 mm) in diameter
- Fabric, $3/_4$" x 8" (2 x 20 cm) (for a scarf); or 1" x $1^1/_2$" (2.5 x 3.5 cm) (for a bowtie)
- Template

Winter Welcome Sign

Apply either a red or a white base coat of paint to the spoons and paint the plywood green. Then make the holes. For the Santa Clauses, place the holes in the handles 7" (18 cm) apart; for the snowman and snow-woman, place the holes 5¼" (13 cm) apart. Pierce one white spoon ⅛" (3 mm) from the rim (where the fringe will be). Pierce all corners of the sign. Paint the face areas of the red spoons with beige paint.

Snowman and Snow-woman

Center a 4" (10 cm) wire around a $2^3/_4$" (7 cm) bunch of abaca fiber and wrap it twice, securing with a knot. Put one wire end through the hole in the forehead and twist together with the other end at the back. Trim the ends. For the snow-woman, place a 4" (10 cm) bunch of abaca fiber around the handle, wrap the 6" (15 cm) wire around it twice, and twist the ends together at the back. Sketch the mouth lightly with a pencil and position the eyes. Trace the mouth with a felt-tip pen and redden the cheeks with a pencil. Add the noses and wobbly eyes and cut the hair into shape.

Santa Clauses

Make the poster board hats and paint them with red acrylic paint to get an even color. Glue the hat to the upper bowl's rim, then add the hat seam, beards, and pompom (all made from poster board). Apply the structural snow paint with a toothpick. Glue the nose and the wobbly eyes in place. Paint on the corners of the mouth and redden the cheeks with a pencil. Brush the mustache with structural snow paint and then glue it on.

To assemble, place the wooden spoons so the holes are exactly aligned, thread the 10" (25 cm) wires halfway through the holes, and twist the ends together at the back. Place the sign in the middle, thread the wire ends through the sign's holes, and twist together again. Wind the hanging wire around a wooden skewer, $^1/_8$" (3 mm) long. Pull the spring off the skewer, stretching the coils slightly apart, thread the ends through the upper frame holes, and twist them together. Use a hole punch to pierce the hearts; thread the wires halfway through the upper holes of the sign. Twist the wire ends into coils with a wooden skewer. Pull the spirals apart slightly and attach the hearts. Paint black veins on the leaves and affix them, with the red wooden beads, to the frame.

Materials for Winter Welcome Sign

- 2 wooden spoons, round bowls, $2^1/_4$" x $12^1/_2$" (5.5 x 31 cm)
- 2 wooden spoons, round bowls, $1^3/_4$" x $9^1/_2$" (4.5 x 24 cm)
- Plywood, $^1/_8$" (3 mm) thick, 6" x $3^1/_2$" (15 x 9 cm) (for the sign)
- Poster board: white, red, dark green
- Matte acrylic paint: red, beige, dark green
- Structural snow paint
- 6 wobbly eyes, about $^1/_8$" (5 mm) in diameter
- 16 wooden beads, about $^1/_4$" (8 mm) in diameter: red
- 1 wooden bead, about $^1/_2$" (12 mm) in diameter (cut in half with a cutter): red
- Abaca fiber: black
- Lacquered wire, about $^1/_{16}$" (0.4 mm) in diameter: black
  4" (10 cm) (head snowman)
  6" (15 cm) (head snow-woman)
  4" x 10" (10 x 25 cm) (frame corners)
  20" (50 cm) (hanger)
  2" x 8" (5 x 20 cm) (hearts)
- Template

Elk Advent Calendar

Apply a base coat of paint to the spoon and ears. Glue the red tongue onto the beige lower jaw and attach from the back to the muzzle. Fill in the nostrils with a pencil. Glue the muzzle, the wobbly eyes, and the antlers to the spoon. Attach the ears at the back. Pierce each spoon four times: 1¼" (3 cm) and 1⅕" (4 cm) away from the end of the handle, and again at 6½" (16 cm) and 16½" (17 cm) away from the end of the handle. Place the handles on top of each other. Bend the wires into a U-shape and thread them from above through the two sets of holes. Twist the wire ends together at the back and shorten. Tie the woolen string to the wire eye. Apply the structural snow paint and let dry. Fold the little pockets in the middle and glue the edges together.

Cut out the hanging holes with a hole punch. Add the numbers and seams, including on the scarves, with puff paint. Set the puff paint with a hair dryer. Attach the little pockets with yarn, tie on the scarves, and add the poster board holly leaves. Glue together the star and attach to the calender with yarn.

Materials for Elk Advent Calendar

- 2 wooden spoons, round bowls, 2¼" x 12½" (5.5 x 31 cm)
- Poster board: sand, beige, red, green, brown
- Matte acrylic paint with structural effects: brown
- Structural snow paint
- 4 oval wobbly eyes, about 0.3" (8 mm) in diameter
- Felt: green, cut to the following dimensions:
  1¼" x 17¾" (3 x 45 cm) (scarves)
  2" x 4¾" (5 x 12 cm), 2¼" x 7" (5.5 x 18 cm),
  1½" x 4¾" (4 x 12 cm), 2¾" x 5½" (7 x 14 cm)
  (24 pockets altogether)
- Puff paint: red
- Yarn: red
- 2 pieces of floral wire, about ¹⁄₃₂" (0.65 mm) in diameter, 8" (20 cm) long
- Hair dryer
- Template

Tip

The pockets will be sturdier if you sew them together with a sewing machine.

Cookie Frieda

Pierce the tip of the spoon and apply a white base coat of paint. Sketch the mouth and attach the wobbly eyes. Place cotton wool on the round piece of fabric and push it through the spoon's hole from the back. Glue the edges of the fabric to the back of the spoon. Tie a piece of wire tightly around a bunch of raffia, leaving about $3\frac{1}{2}$" (9 cm) to one side. Place the tie over the hole made earlier and thread a piece of wire from the front through the hole. Secure it by twisting both wire ends together at the back. Divide the raffia into two strands. To make the pigtails, tie the left strand with wire at about 2" (5 cm) and the right one at about $3\frac{1}{2}$" (9 cm). Cover the wire with ribbon bows and attach the inscribed heart.

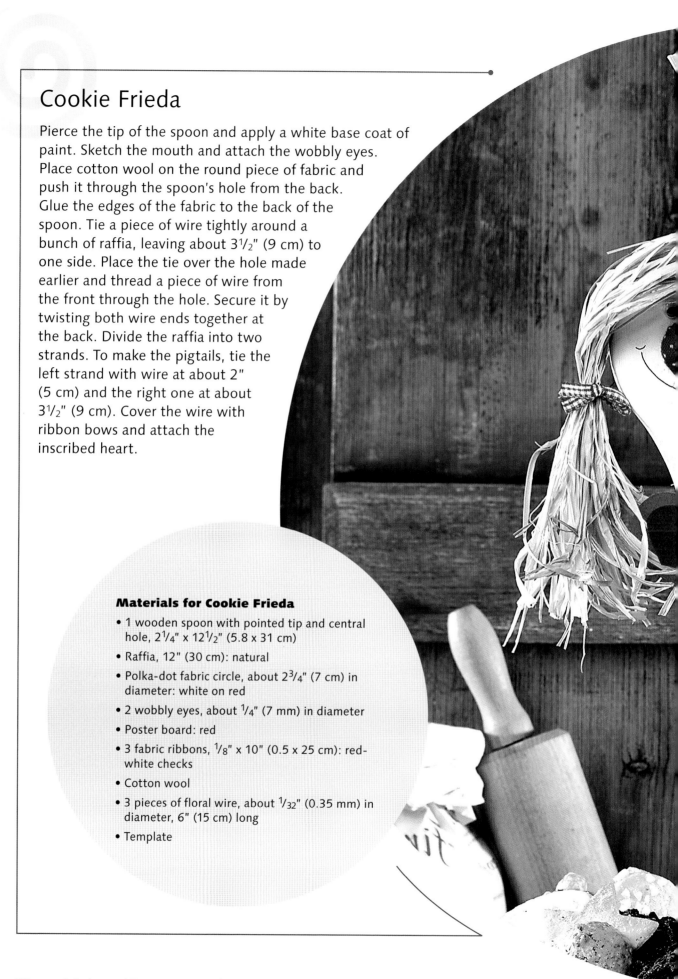

Materials for Cookie Frieda

- 1 wooden spoon with pointed tip and central hole, $2\frac{1}{4}$" x $12\frac{1}{2}$" (5.8 x 31 cm)
- Raffia, 12" (30 cm): natural
- Polka-dot fabric circle, about $2\frac{3}{4}$" (7 cm) in diameter: white on red
- 2 wobbly eyes, about $\frac{1}{4}$" (7 mm) in diameter
- Poster board: red
- 3 fabric ribbons, $\frac{1}{8}$" x 10" (0.5 x 25 cm): red-white checks
- Cotton wool
- 3 pieces of floral wire, about $\frac{1}{32}$" (0.35 mm) in diameter, 6" (15 cm) long
- Template

Snow Didi

Apply a white base coat of paint to the spoon and then paint the face. Fold the abaca fiber in half and glue it to the back. Attach the ears and cut the hair into shape. Dab the white dots onto the bow tie with a wooden skewer. Glue on the wooden beads as buttons.

Three Men in the Snow

Glue the hatband and the patches to the front of the hats and attach the hair to the back. Paint the raclette spatulas white, let dry, and then glue the hats to them. Paint the faces and glue on the noses. Glue on the bow tie and the sign with the hands attached. Tie on the scarf and the neckerchief. Tie the small piece of fabric into a bow tie with wire and glue onto the hat. Apply structural snow paint with a toothpick.

Cut the Styrofoam sheet into shape with a coping saw. Wind aluminum wire twice around a tea light, creating a spiral that decreases in diameter, and ends with a straight section of wire. Carefully make incisions in the Styrofoam with a knife, insert the snowmen into them, and push the candleholders straight into the Styrofoam.

Materials for Three Men in the Snow

- 3 raclette spatulas, $1^1/_2$" x 5" (3.7 x 13 cm)
- Poster board: yellow, orange, red, brown, black, blue, white
- Structural snow paint
- Abaca fiber: black
- Grass fiber: yellow, brown
- Fabric: blue-white check
- 1 piece of fabric, $1^1/_8$" x 6" (3 x 15 cm): red-white check
- 1 piece of fabric, $^3/_4$" x 1" (2 x 2.5 cm): red-white check
- Flower wire, about $^1/_{32}$" (0.35 mm) in diameter
- 4 tea lights
- 4 aluminum wires, about $^1/_{16}$" (2 mm) in diameter, 24" to 32" (60 to 80 cm) long
- Template

Reindeer

Apply a gray base coat of paint to the spoon and let dry. Glue the tongue to the white lower jaw and then glue the jaw from the back onto the muzzle. Glue on the nose. With a black felt-tip pen, draw a vertical line to separate the muzzle. Glue the white inner ear pieces onto the gray ears.

Glue the muzzle from the front onto the spoon and add the white hair and the wobbly eyes. Attach the antlers and ears from the back. Apply structural snow paint with a bristle brush. Tie one end of the long strand of yarn to the bottom of the handle, wind it in a spiral pattern around the handle, and tie it securely about 1¼" (3 cm) below the muzzle. Wind the short strand of yarn around this part of the handle, tie securely, and add a wooden bead to each end, securing each bead with a knot.

With a black felt-tip pen, draw the veins on the leaves. Add structural snow paint to the edges. Attach the leaves between the wooden beads.

Materials for One Reindeer
(Three shown at left)

- 1 wooden spoon, round bowl, 2⅛" x 12½" (5.5 x 31 cm)
- Poster board: gray, sand, white, red, black, green
- Matte acrylic paint: gray
- Structural snow paint
- 2 wobbly eyes, about ½" (12 mm) in diameter
- 2 wooden beads, about ½" (10 mm) in diameter: red
- 1 strand of yarn, 6" (15 cm) long: red
- 1 strand of yarn, 28" (70 cm) long: red
- Template

Materials for Pair of Gnomes

- 2 wooden spoons, long oval bowl, 2⅛" x 12½" (5.5 x 31 cm)
- Poster board: beige, yellow, green, red, white
- Matte acrylic paint: red
- 4 untreated wooden beads, about ½" (10 mm) in diameter
- 2 wooden beads, about ¼" (6 mm) in diameter: red
- 4 wooden beads, about ½" (10 mm) in diameter: red
- 1 wooden bead, about ½" (8 mm) in diameter: red
- 2 chenille wires, 5½" (14 cm) long: red
- Felt: red, light brown
- Cotton wool
- Thread: red
- 2 small metal bells, about ½" (10 mm) in diameter
- Template

Pair of Gnomes

With the drilling template, pierce both spoons accordingly, and then apply a red base coat of paint to all sides. Paint the face on the beige poster board head. Halve a ½" (10 mm) red wooden bead with a cutter, and glue on one half as a nose. Glue the head onto the spoon. Place the bottom rim of the felt hat around the forehead and the spoon, and glue into position; the hat should stay partly open at the back. Attach the little bell just below of the tip of the hat with a needle and thread.

To make the arms, thread the chenille wire through the holes from the back and attach a wooden bead to each end. To make the bag, fold over the felt along the dotted line, apply glue to the dotted area, and glue it together (see template). Open the felt tube slightly at the bottom end, add a dab of glue to the edges, and push together. Fill the bag with cotton wool, add the twig, and then tie the bag closed. Add a wooden bead to each string end and secure the beads with several knots. Assemble the sign as shown and attach to the spoons.

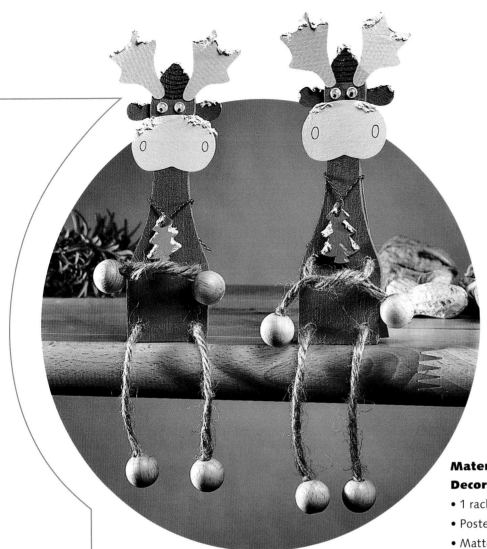

Elk Table Edge Decoration

Drill the holes as shown in the template. Paint the tip of the spoon either green or red to make the hats. Paint the rest of the raclette spatula and the poster board ears brown. Decorate the hats with black felt-tip pen lines.

Glue the antlers, muzzle, and wobbly eyes to the front of the spoon. Add the ears at the back. Apply structural snow paint with a toothpick. Punch a hole in the poster board Christmas tree, add structural snow paint, and let dry. Thread cord or wire through the tree hole and tie around the elk's neck.

To make the arms, thread the cord from the front through one of the holes and then again from the back through the other hole. Glue a wooden bead to each end. Make the legs exactly the same way. Finish by gluing a small strip of cardboard at the back of the neck to help prop up the elk.

Materials for One Elk Table Edge Decoration (two shown)

- 1 raclette spatula, $1^1/_2$" x 5" (3.7 x 13 cm)
- Poster board: sand, brown, green
- Matte acrylic paint with structural effects: brown
- Matte acrylic paint: red or green
- Structural snow paint
- 2 wobbly eyes, about $1/_8$" (5 mm)
- 4 untreated wooden beads, about $1/_2$" (15 mm)
- 1 jute cord, about $1/_{16}$" (3.5 mm) x $6^1/_2$" (16 cm): natural
- 1 jute cord, about $1/_{16}$" (3.5 mm) x 8" (20 cm): natural
- Thin cord or floral wire, 8" (20 cm)
- Template

Wish List Angel

Make a drilling template and make four holes for the arms and legs. Paint the bowl and feet blue and paint the handle gold. Paint stars on the bowl with glitter glue. Double the gold cord and thread it through the holes from the back to make the legs and arms. Tie the wooden beads and puppet feet to the cord. Make a hole in the forehead about $1/4$" (5 mm) away from the edge. Tie the raffia bunch in the middle with a piece of wire. Thread the wire from the front through the forehead hole and twist the two ends together at the back. With your fingers, dab glitter glue on the wings and stars. Cut the wish-list sign with deckle-edge scissors. Inscribe the sign, roll it up, secure with the clothespins, and attach to the angel.

Materials for Wish List Angel

- 1 wooden spoon, oval bowl, 2" x 8" (5 x 40 cm)
- Poster board: shiny gold, beige
- Matte acrylic paint: blue, gold
- 2 untreated wooden beads, about $1/3$" (15 mm) in diameter
- 2 puppet feet, 1" x $1^1/4$" (24 x 32 mm)
- Raffia, $6^1/2$" (16 cm): rust brown
- 2 gold cords, about $1/4$" (8 mm) in diameter, 20" (50 cm) long
- Brass wire, about $1/16$" (3 mm) in diameter, 4" (10 cm) long
- Glitter glue: gold
- Thin poster board, 3" x 4" (8 x 10 cm): white
- Deckle-edge scissors
- 2 miniature clothespins, 1" (2.5 cm) long: gold (or painted gold)
- Template

Gift-Giving Angel

Make a hole in the forehead about $1/8$" (3 mm) from the edge of the bowl. Paint the bowl beige and draw the face. Wind the 8" (20 cm) length of brass wire around a rounded wooden skewer to make a spiral. Thread one end through the forehead hole and twist into place at the back. Attach the star to the other end. Center and tie a piece of the 4" (10 cm) brass wire centrally around the golden cord. Thread a wire through the hole from the front and twist together with the other end at the back of the head. Make hair bows with single threads pulled from the 6" (15 cm) decorative cord. Punch a hole in the leatherlike paper and decorate with glitter glue. Glue the leatherlike paper dress to the spoon. Thread the arm string from the front through the armhole, pull it around the spoon, and pass it through the other armhole from the back. Glue a wooden bead to each end. Glue the wings to the back of the spoon. Wind the leftover wire around a pen to make a spiral and attach it below the dress. Wrap the present with gold crepe paper and secure each end with a bow using the decorative cord. Tie the present around the handle.

Tip

This angel can also hold a gift voucher or paper money.

Materials for Gift-Giving Angel

- 1 wooden spoon, round bowl, $1^3/4$" x $9^1/2$" (4.5 x 24 cm)
- Poster board: beige
- Leatherlike paper: burgundy red
- Shiny poster board: gold
- Crepe paper: gold
- Matte acrylic paint: beige
- Glitter glue: gold
- 2 untreated wooden beads, about $1/2$" (15 mm)
- 20 cords, about $1/4$" (8 mm) in diameter, $6^1/4$" (16 cm) long: gold
- 1 decorative cord, about $1/8$" (4 mm) in diameter, $5^1/2$" (14 cm) long: burgundy red
- 2 decorative cords, about $1/16$" (2 mm) in diameter, 8" (20 cm) long: burgundy red
- 1 decorative cord, about $1/16$" (2 mm) in diameter, 16" (40 cm) long: burgundy red
- 1 decorative cord, about $1/16$" (2 mm) in diameter, 6" (15 cm) long: color of choice
- 2 pieces of brass wire, about $1/8$" (4 mm) in diameter, 8" (20 cm) long
- 2 pieces of brass wire, about $1/8$" (4 mm) in diameter, 4" (10 cm) long
- 1 rounded wooden skewer, about $1/8$" (3 mm) (for adding paint detail)
- Template

Penguin

Make four holes in the spoon—three according to the drilling template and one for the notepad 2½" (6 cm) below the leg holes. Paint the hat green and then paint the rest of the spoon black; let dry. Paint the chest and belly area white. Glue on the beak, wobbly eyes, wings, and pompom. Thread the cord for the legs from the back through the holes. Add one wooden bead and one foot to each end and secure in place with a knot. Fold the wire for the notepad in half. Thread both ends from the back through the hole. Spread the ends of the wire and hang the spiral notepad from them, folding back the tips to secure the wire.

Polar Bear

Make the drilling template and then make the holes for the legs and arms. Paint the spoon and wooden beads white. Thread the ends of the cotton wool string from the back through the holes. Glue a bead to each end. Glue the nose and wobbly eyes to the head and attach the head to the body. Wind the wire around a wooden skewer, pull off the spiral, stretch it slightly, wind it around the neck, and attach the heart to it. Glue on the sign.

Bear with a Red Hat

Paint the tip of the bowl red and apply a brown base coat to the rest of the spoon and the ears. Glue the beige inner ears to the ears and glue them to the back. Add the bobble at the back and then glue the muzzle and wobbly eyes at the front. Apply structural snow paint and tie on the fringed scarf.

Materials for Bear with a Red Hat

- 1 wooden spoon with pointed tip, $2^1/_8$" x $12^1/_2$" (5.5 x 31 cm)
- Poster board: beige, black, brown
- Structural craft paint: brown
- Matte acrylic paint: red
- Structural snow paint
- 2 wobbly eyes, about $1/_4$" (5 mm) in diameter
- Felt, $3/_4$" x 8" (2 x 20 cm): red
- Template

Materials for Reindeer 2

- 1 raclette spatula, $1\frac{1}{2}$" x 4" (3.7 x 13 cm)
- Poster board: sand, gray, white, and green or red
- Structural craft paint: gray
- Matte acrylic paint: green or red
- Structural snow paint
- 2 wobbly eyes, about $\frac{1}{8}$" (5 mm) in diameter
- Lacquer wire, about $\frac{1}{32}$" (0.4 mm) in diameter, 4" (10 cm) long: black
- Small metal bell, about $\frac{1}{2}$" (16 mm) in diameter: red
- Template

Tip

Without the support and with a hole drilled in the hat for a piece of string or a wire hook, the reindeer can also be used as a Christmas tree ornament.

Reindeer 2

To make the hat, paint the tip of the spoon red or green. Apply a gray base coat of paint to the rest of the raclette spatula, muzzle, and ears; let dry. Then paint the reindeer chest white. Decorate the hat with a black felt-tip pen. Glue the antlers, the muzzle, and the wobbly eyes to the front of the spatula. Glue the ears to the back. Apply structural snow paint with a toothpick. To support the back, glue a narrow piece of gray card to the back of the neck. Hang the little bell around the neck with a piece of wire.

Fir Tree Spoon

Apply a green base coat of paint to the wooden spoon. (You may also want to paint the green poster board tree to get the same green color.) Add the nose and wobbly eyes and then draw the mouth. Glue the candle to the back of the head and then glue the head onto the tree. Paint the flame with a felt-tip pen. Apply structural snow paint with a paintbrush and toothpick. Tie on a raffia bow and some pieces of fir with wire.

Materials for Fir Tree Spoon

- 1 wooden spoon, round bowl, $2^1/_4$" x $12^1/_2$" (5.5 x 31 cm)
- Poster board: green, red, yellow
- Matte acrylic paint: green
- Structural snow paint
- Wooden bead, about $1/_2$" (12 mm) in diameter (cut in half with a cutter): red
- 2 oval wobbly eyes, about $1/_2$" (10 mm) in diameter
- Raffia: natural
- Flower wire, about $1/_{32}$" (6 mm)
- Template

Angel

Make a hole ¹/₁₆" (3 mm) from the tip of the spoon. Paint the head and neck beige or brown and the rest of the spatula white. Attach one end of the hanging wire in the forehead hole. Draw the face and decorate the dress with glitter glue. Tie a bunch of angel hair, about 3" to 4" (8 to 10 cm) long, in the middle with a short piece of wire. Thread the wire end from the front through the forehead hole and twist together with the other end at the back. Hook a star to each wire end. With your fingers, dab glitter glue on the wings and the large and small stars. Attach the wings and the large star with the hands to the angel.

Tip

These angels will also look beautiful as Christmas tree ornaments, or placed in a seasonal flower arrangement.

Materials for Angel

- 1 raclette spatula, 1¹/₂" x 5" (3.7 x 13 cm)
- Poster board: white, beige
- Shiny poster board: gold
- Matte acrylic paint: beige or brown
- Brass wire, about ¹/₃₂" (0.3 mm) in diameter, 12" (30 cm) long
- Brass wire, about ¹/₃₂" (0.3 mm) in diameter, 8" (20 cm) long
- Angel hair: gold
- Glitter glue: gold
- Template

Skiing Penguin

Make a hole in the handle of the spatula, paint the tip either red or blue, and then paint the rest of the spatula black. Let dry and paint the chest and belly area white. Glue the smaller white piece of poster board to red or green ski goggles and attach the wobbly eyes to that. Attach the goggles below the hat and the beak below the goggles. Glue the wings to the back. Fold over the tip of the wings, and then attach the painted wooden skewers as ski poles. Score the back part of the feet along the dotted line, fold over, and glue on the skis. Attach the ski bindings. Attach the ends of the feet that stick out to the back of the spatula. Fix the signs and apply the structural snow paint. Wind a piece of wire around the pompom and then thread the other end through the hole to make the hanger. Make a spiral by winding the wire around a pencil.

Materials for One Skiing Penguin (two shown)

- 1 raclette spatula, 1¹⁄₈" x 1¹⁄₂" (3 x 3.7 cm)
- Poster board: black, white, red, and blue or green
- Matte acrylic paint: black, red or blue
- Structural snow paint
- 2 wobbly eyes, about ¹⁄₄" (7 mm) in diameter
- 1 pompom: red or green
- 2 rounded wooden skewers, about ¹⁄₁₆" (2 mm) in diameter, 2¹⁄₂" (6 cm) long
- Lacquer wire, about ¹⁄₈" (0.4 mm) in diameter, 12" (30 cm) long: black
- Template

Thermometer and Snow Gauge

Make the hole for the hair and the thermometer mounting. Paint the spoon white, draw the face, and add the rubber parts. Position the aluminum wire over the rim of the thermometer spoon bowl and glue into place. Wind the chenille wire into a spiral and add as earmuffs. Thread the two lacquer wire pieces halfway through the forehead hole, twist together to hold in place, and then wind all ends around a pencil to make spirals.

For the thermometer: Bend each piece of sticking wire $^1/_8$" (0.5 cm) from one end to a 90° angle. Stick the thermometer onto the wire. For the snow gauge: Paint on the scale, taking into account the thickness of the piece of wood the spoon will stand in. Add structural snow paint. File an angle on the edges of the footboard, and then apply a white base coat of paint. Drill the hole in the footboard and glue the snowman in place. Knit a scarf from the red yarn that is 1" x 6" (2.5 x 15 cm). (You can substitute a strip of felt or other thick fabric of the same dimensions.) Wrap the scarf around the snowman's neck and secure with a knot.

Materials for Snow Gauge

- 1 wooden spoon, round bowl, $1^3/_4$" x $11^1/_4$" (4.5 x 28.5 cm)
- Moss rubber: orange, red, black, blue
- Weatherproof acrylic paint: white
- Structural snow paint
- 1 wooden board, $^3/_4$" (18 mm) thick, measuring 3" x 3" (8 x 8 cm) or 6" x 6" (15 x 15 cm)
- Template

Materials for Thermometer

- 1 wooden spoon, round bowl, $1^3/_4$" x $11^1/_4$" (4.5 x 28.5 cm)
- Adhesive-backed rubber: orange
- Weatherproof acrylic paint: white
- Structural snow paint
- 1 thermometer, $1^1/_2$" x $6^1/_2$" (3.5 x 16 cm)
- 2 chenille wires, $3^1/_2$" (9 cm): blue
- Yarn: red
- Knitting needles
- Aluminum wire, about $^1/_{16}$" (2 mm) in diameter, $3^1/_2$" (9 cm) long: blue
- 2 lacquer wires, about $^1/_{32}$" (0.4 mm) in diameter, $5^1/_2$" (14 cm) long: black
- 2 pieces of sticking wire, about $^1/_{16}$" (1 mm) in diameter, $1^1/_4$" (3 cm) long
- 1 rounded wooden skewer, about $^1/_{10}$" (3 mm) (for adding paint detail)
- Template

Lucky Pig

Make a drilling template and drill the holes. Apply a pink base coat of paint to the wooden beads and the broad end of the spatula. Thread the cord through and tie on the beads. Draw the face and then add the snout. To give the snout depth, underlay it with three pink board dots, about 3/4" (2 cm). Attach the inscribed sign with the clothespins and glue on the clover and ladybug.

Materials for Lucky Pig
- 1 wooden spatula, 2 1/4" x 12" (5.8 x 30 cm)
- Poster board: pink, white, green
- Craft paint: pink
- 2 untreated wooden beads, about 3/4" (1.8 cm) in diameter
- 2 miniature wooden clothespins, 1 3/4" (4.5 cm) in diameter: red
- 2 decorative ladybugs, about 3/4" (2 cm) in diameter
- Cotton wool cord, about 1/8" (3 mm) in diameter, 10 3/4" (27 cm) long: pink
- Template

Materials for Slidy Bug
- 1 wooden spoon with pointed tip, 2" x 12" (5 x 30 cm)
- Poster board: black, white, red
- 7 sticky dots, about 1/4" (8 mm) in diameter: black
- Matte acrylic paint, red, light green
- 1 chenille wire, 5 1/2" (14 cm) in diameter: black
- 2 chenille wires, 4 1/4" (11 cm) in diameter: black
- Lacquer wire, about 1/16" (0.4 mm) in diameter, 4" (10 cm) long: black
- 2 wooden beads, about 1/4" (6 mm) in diameter: black

Slidy Bug
(opposite, bottom left, in photo)

Apply the base coat of paint as shown. Make a black line to indicate the wings and add the sticky dots. Attach the pearls to the wire ends and glue the other ends to the assembled head. Glue the head to the body. Add the legs at the back of the body and glue to sign to the handle.

Chimneysweep
(bottom right, in photo)

Make a drilling template and make the holes. Paint the spatula beige and black, let dry, and then draw the face. Add a clover, heart, and hatband to the front of the top hat and add the grass fiber as hair at the back. Glue on the hat. Thread the chenille wire through the holes to make the arms and legs. To make the feet, bend back the wire ends at 1¹/₂" (4 cm) and wind the wire around to make the heel. Tie on the felt scarf with fringe cut into the ends.

Materials for Chimneysweep
- 1 raclette spatula, 1¹/₂" x 5" (3.7 x 13 cm)
- Poster board: black, red, green, white
- Matte acrylic paint: black, beige
- Grass fiber: yellow
- Felt, ³/₄" x 8" (2 x 20 cm): red
- 1 chenille wire, 6¹/₂" (16 cm): black
- 1 chenille wire, 13¹/₂" (34 cm): black
- Template

Materials for Lucky New Year Charms
- 1 wooden spoon with pointed tip, 2" x 12" (5 x 30 cm)
- Poster board: red, white, black, green
- Matte acrylic paint: light green, black
- 2 chenille wires, 4³/₄" (12 cm)
- 1 chenille wire, 5¹/₂" (14 cm)
- Yarn, 24" (60 cm) long: red
- Fabric, 2¹/₂" x 2¹/₂" (6 x 6 cm): red with white dots
- Template

Lucky New Year Charms (top, in photo)

Make a drilling template, then drill the holes. Paint the spoon as shown. Thread the chenille wire from the back through the holes. Glue on the wings, the sign, and the head. Attach the thread to the bottom of the handle, wind it around, and thread it through the sign. Attach the fabric to one leg (by folding over the chenille wire so it holds the fabric) and bend all legs into shape.

The Three Kings

Paint the bowl and a bit of the handle. Cut the wooden bead in half to make the nose and paint it the same color. Glue on the nose and the wobbly eyes. Draw the face and the eyebrows. To make the hair for the blue king, cut a 2³/₄" (7 cm) piece from the doll's hair braid, loosen it, and glue it to the head. For the green king, make a center part by tying a piece of thread around the middle of the thirty strands of black thread.

Glue the hair to the head. Cut out the crowns from the foil with scissors, bend them around the head, and decorate with glitter glue. To make the turban, fold the tissue paper into a ³/₄" (2 cm) strip. Apply glitter glue to the red turban piece and add this first to the back of the head. Glue on the ears and then wind the tissue ribbon around the head and glue into place. Add golden glitter glue dots.

All robes have the same basic shape. For the red robe, punch holes into both bottom sides. Decorate the robes with gold trim, then place around the handle and knot together with a gold cord. Wind the chenille arm wire once around the neck, twist the ends together, and add a wooden bead (untreated or painted) to each end. Push the robe over the arms slightly.

Tip

These kings are classic gift bearers for all sorts of presents, including paper money, wrapped trinkets, and jewelry.

Materials for The Three Kings

- 3 wooden spoons, round bowls, 2" x 10³/₄" (5 x 27.5 cm)
- Poster board: red, blue, green
- Shiny poster board: gold
- Matte acrylic paint: beige, ochre, brown
- 2 untreated wooden beads, about ¹/₂" (12 mm) in diameter (cut in half with a cutter)
- 6 wobbly eyes, about ¹/₄" (5 mm) in diameter
- 2 pieces of gold trim, ¹/₄" x 3¹/₂" (0.5 x 9 cm)
- 3 pieces of gold trim, ¹/₄" x 5¹/₂" (0.5 x 14 cm)
- Cord, about ¹/₁₆" (0.8 mm): gold
- 1 chenille wire, 10" (25 cm): red
- 1 chenille wire, 10" (25 cm): blue
- 1 chenille wire, 10" (25 cm): green
- Doll's hair braid: black
- 30 cotton wool threads, about ¹/₁₆" (1 mm) in diameter, each 6" (15 cm) long: black
- Tissue paper
- Glitter glue: gold
- Metal foil, 0.15 mm thick: gold
- Template

Star

Apply a yellow base coat of paint to the spoon, let dry, and then draw the face. Wind each 6" (15 cm) piece of wire around the wooden skewer, pull off, stretch, and hook a small red star to each end. Glue the abaca fiber to the back of the head to make the hair. Let dry and then cut into the desired hairstyle. Attach the ears, star spirals, and large star. Wind the wire a few times around the neck, twist the ends together, and then make it into a spiral and add a small star to each end.

Materials for Star

- 1 wooden spoon, round bowl, $2^{1}/_{4}$" x $15^{1}/_{2}$" (5.5 x 39.5 cm)
- Poster board: yellow, red
- Matte acrylic paint: yellow
- Abaca fiber: black
- 3 pieces of lacquer wire, about $^{1}/_{16}$" (0.4 mm) in diameter, 6" (15 cm) long: black
- 3 pieces of lacquer wire, about $^{1}/_{16}$" (0.4 mm) in diameter, 18" (45 cm) long: black
- 1 rounded wooden skewer, about $^{1}/_{8}$" (3 mm)
- Template

Spoon Buddies for Children's Rooms

The wooden spoons are leaving the kitchen drawer once again and are moving—brightly decorated—into the kids' rooms. They are to be seen in cheerful colors, lovingly made into frame monsters, hairgrip princesses, bulletin boards, foxes, pencil clowns, and notepad elephants, creating a happy atmosphere. All you need is wood, paper, wire, paint, and of course a wooden spoon and you can make funny and cheerful things. Surprise your child with a wild wooden spoon! You will find projects here for both boys and girls.

— Tamara Franke
Contributing Author

> **Tip**
>
> Put small treats—letters, notes, candy, and so on—in the pot.

Betty, Petty, and Netty Bear Door Sign

Pierce the top corners of the balsa wood sign with a needle. Thread the string through and tie at the back. Paint the bears as shown. Paint the poster board to match the base colors, cut out the ears, and attach them at the back. Attach the painted wooden beads as hands to the chenille wire arms and attach them just below the bowl.

Attach the bears and the clay pot to the green raclette spatula. When you attach the baby bear, make sure the string of the sign can be draped freely over the head. The sign can be turned over depending on the mood.

> **Tip**
>
> The letters and words can designed on the computer and transferred like any other template onto wood with tracing paper.

Materials for Betty, Petty, and Netty Bear Door Sign

- 2 wooden spoons, round bowls, about 1³/₄" x 12³/₄" (4.7 x 32 cm)
- 1 wooden spoon, round bowl, about 1³/₄" x 7³/₄" (4.5 x 19.5 cm)
- 3 raclette spatulas, 5" (13 cm) long
- 1 clay pot, about 2¹/₂" (6 cm)
- Matte acrylic paint: light pink, bright pink, yellow, lime, emerald green, light green, black, cappuccino, light blue, honeydew, orange
- 1 chenille wire, about 4³/₄" (12 cm): pink
- 1 chenille wire, 6" (15 cm): yellow
- 1 chenille wire, 6" (15 cm): green
- 2 half-pierced untreated wooden beads, about ³/₄" (2 cm) in diameter
- 4 half-pierced untreated wooden beads, about 1" (2.5 cm) in diameter
- Poster board: white
- Balsa wood, 2¹/₂" x 4¹/₂" (6 x 11.5 cm)
- String, about 6" (15 cm) long: natural
- Template

Materials for Enchanted Frog Prince Penholder

- 1 wooden spoon, round bowl, about 2" x 12³/₄" (5.4 x 32 cm)
- Poster board: white
- Matte acrylic paint: kelly green, sky blue, gold, pink, ochre, dark blue, dark green
- Moss rubber: red
- 1 untreated wooden bead, about ³/₄" (2 cm) in diameter
- 1 chenille wire, 3" (8 cm): apple green
- 1 chenille wire, 7" (18 cm): apple green
- 2 aluminum wires, about ¹/₁₆" (2 mm) in diameter, 4³/₄" (12 cm) long: silver
- Paper towel cardboard tube
- 1 round wooden board, about ³/₄" (2 cm) thick, 5¹/₂" (14 cm) in diameter
- Template

Materials for Frog Freida Thermometer

- 1 wooden spoon, round bowl, about 2" x 12¹/₈" (5.2 x 30.5 cm)
- Poster board: white
- 1 chenille wire, 3" (8 cm): apple green
- 1 chenille wire, 7" (18 cm): apple green
- Matte acrylic paint: lemon yellow, pink, red, light blue
- Glitter paint: blue-turquoise
- Binding wire, about ¹/₈" (0.5 mm) in diameter, 2" (5 cm) long: orange
- Thermometer, 1¹/₈" x 5" (3 x 13.5 cm)
- Template

Frog Frieda and the Enchanted Frog Prince Penholder and Thermometer

for the penholder

With a coping saw, shorten the handle to 6³/₄" (17 cm) and paint the spoon. Attach the painted poster board crown and the moss rubber tongue with hot glue. Attach the eyes with glue pads. Using the shorter piece of chenille wire for the arms and the longer one for the legs, attach both at the back of the spoon. Attach golden beads to the ends as hands and feet.

Cut the paper towel roll into three pieces, two measuring 1³/₄" (4.5 cm) and one 4³/₄" (12 cm). Then paint them: paint the buckets dark brown and apply some ochre lines for texture. Apply the brick pattern to the well with a fine brush or toothpick. Make two holes in each bucket, bend the wire into handles, and put them through the holes. Secure with hot glue.

Attach the cardboard tubes to the painted wooden board with hot glue. Glue the wooden spoon behind the highest tube and bend the arms and legs into shape.

for the thermometer

Cut the binding wire in half, fold each piece in half, and glue behind the eyes as eyelashes. Attach the eyes to the painted spoon with glue pads. Using the shorter piece of chenille wire for the arms and the longer piece for the legs, attach them to the back of the bowl with hot glue. Attach the hand and feet to the wire ends and bend the wire into shape. Decorate the light blue handle with glitter glue and attach the thermometer with hot glue or wood glue.

Tom Bluenose Letter Holder

With a coping saw, shorten the spoon to $8^1/_2$" (21 cm). Cut the hut, roof, and sign from balsa wood and varnish the floor, fence, and hut. Let dry; decorate as shown. Draw slats on the bigger board with a colored pencil and assemble all the pieces with wood glue.

Paint and decorate the spoon. Attach the paper ears and the painted wire pieces (hair) to the back of the bowl. Attach the spoon at the back of the fence. Secure the paws with glue pad. Attach the letter to the mouth with paint and attach it to the paws with glue pads.

Paint the clay pot and put a stamp and paperclip holder next to the dog hut. Decorate with a paper bone.

Materials for Tom Bluenose Letter Holder

- 1 wooden spoon, round bowl, about 2" x $12^1/_8$" (5.2 x 30.5 cm)
- Balsa wood, $^1/_{16}$" to $^1/_8$" (3 to 5 mm) x $5^1/_4$" x 8" (13.5 x 20 cm)
- Balsa wood, $^1/_{16}$" to $^1/_8$" (3 to 5 mm) x $2^1/_2$" x 4" (6 x 10 cm)
- Balsa wood, $^1/_{16}$" to $^1/_8$" (3 to 5 mm) x $4^3/_4$" x $5^1/_4$" (12 x 13.5 cm)
- Antique-effect varnish
- 1 clay pot, about $1^1/_2$" (4 cm) in diameter
- Matte acrylic paint: apricot, ochre, dark brown, emerald green, sky blue, pink, orange, beige
- Poster board: white
- Aluminum wire, about $^1/_{16}$" (2 mm) in diameter: silver
- Template

Materials for Bluebeard and Stripy Shirt Treasure Chest

- 2 wooden spoons, round bowls, about $2\frac{1}{4}$" x $12\frac{3}{4}$" (5.2 x 32 cm)
- 2 pieces of sisal wire, about $\frac{1}{2}$" (1 cm) thick, $9\frac{1}{2}$" (24 cm) long
- Matte acrylic paint: beige, pink, gold, salmon, light brown, sky blue, light blue, ice blue, red, ochre, dark brown
- Poster board: white
- 2 cotton craft balls, about $\frac{1}{2}$" (1.5 cm) in diameter
- Raffia, about 24" (60 cm): medium brown
- Raffia, about $3\frac{1}{2}$" (9 cm): natural
- 1 wooden box, 2" x $3\frac{1}{8}$" x $4\frac{1}{2}$" (5 x 8 x 11 cm)
- Antique varnish or furniture wax: light brown
- 4 wooden disks, about 1" (2.5 cm) in diameter
- 2 tree stands, $\frac{1}{2}$" x $2\frac{3}{4}$" x $3\frac{1}{2}$" (1.5 x 7 x 9 cm)
- Template

Tip

This treasure chest can be used to store light, small things like earrings, coins, or chains. For heavier treasures, drill holes in a larger base and put the chest at the feet of the figures.

Bluebeard and Stripy Shirt Treasure Chest

Varnish the chest and use a fine brush and gold paint to edge the chest. Paint the spoons according the image at right, and use the template provided to create additional components from poster board. Glue on the painted figuring wire as arms and the cotton craft balls as noses.

To make the pirate, glue the ears to the back of the spoon bowl, and the neckerchief and knife to the front. Tie a raffia belt between the shirt and the trousers.

For the pirate captain, use hot glue to attach a brown raffia ponytail to the back of the bowl. Paint the poster board hat, collar, beard, and cuffs, and glue pieces into place as shown.

Put the spoon handles into the tree stands, using glue if necessary. Attach the shoes to the base of the spoon. Bend the pirates' arms into position as shown (or as desired). Glue the treasure chest onto three of the sisal cord arms and glue the wooden disks to the ends, as hands. Attach another wooden disk to the raised arm and glue the sword onto it. (Make sure to paint on the handle detail beforehand!)

Please note: This treasure chest should only be used for small, lightweight trinkets such as earrings, coins, or necklaces. For keeping heavier treasures, set the pirates into a thicker, wider wooden board (for added stability). Drill holes wide enough to accommodate the spoon handles where desired, and stand the chest at their feet.

Pretty Princess Accessories Holder and Jewelry Stand

With a drill, widen the holes of the untreated wooden beads to fit the diameter of the spoon handle. Paint all wooden parts as shown. Dab on the pattern of the collar and cuffs with a cotton swab. Cut the raffia into twenty evenly sized pieces and the curly ribbon into six. Use three pieces of curly ribbon each to tie ten pieces of raffia each. Curl the ribbon further and glue the pigtails to the back of the bowl.

Attach the wooden stick about ³/₄" (2 cm) below the bowl and secure with a nail. Stick the wooden beads to the ends but do not glue them on. This will enable you to take them off to put on smaller rings and trinkets. Paint the gold trim and the bust line onto the paper dress. Then attach the dress to the wooden stick with masking tape and affix the stick to the spoon handle with hot glue.

Attach the die-cut flower decorations to the dress and hair with foam pads. Paint the wooden half-bead, let dry, and attach to the handle. Insert the handle in the tree stand and then glue the bead to the base.

Variation: Tie string between the arms and use miniature clothespins to hang kids' paintings, photographs, or notes.

Materials for Pretty Princess Accessories Holder and Jewelry Stand
- 1 wooden spoon, round bowl, about 2¹/₄" x 12³/₄" (5.7 x 32 cm)
- Matte acrylic paint: beige, orange, pink, light blue, gold, lemon yellow
- Poster board: white
- 2 half-pierced untreated wooden beads, about 1" (2.5 cm) in diameter
- 1 pierced untreated wooden half-bead, about 1¹/₈" (3 cm) in diameter
- Die cut, about ¹/₂" (1.5 cm), daisy pattern
- 1 dowel, about ¹/₂" x 8³/₄" (1.2 x 22 cm)
- Glitter paint: turquoise
- Curly ribbon, about 19" (48 cm): shiny white
- Raffia, about 24" (60 cm): orange
- 1 tree stand, ¹/₂" x 2¹/₂" x 3¹/₂" (1.5 x 6.5 x 9 cm)
- Template

Materials for At Home with the Monsters—Frame or Mirror Decoration

- 1 wooden picture frame, 11" x 13$\frac{1}{8}$" (28 x 33 cm) (outer edges)
- 2 wooden wok spoons, 2$\frac{1}{2}$" x 12" (6.5 x 30 cm)
- Matte acrylic paint: pink, light blue, bright pink, orange, emerald green, sky blue, lemon yellow, red, turquoise, apricot, yellow
- Aluminum wire, about $\frac{1}{16}$" (1 mm) in diameter, 20" (50 cm) long: blue
- Aluminum wire, about $\frac{1}{8}$" (2 mm) in diameter, 4" (10 cm) long: silver
- 1 pompom, about 1$\frac{1}{2}$" (4 cm) in diameter: light green
- Ribbon, $\frac{1}{2}$" x 6" (1 x 15 cm): red-white check
- Chenille wire, 9$\frac{1}{2}$" (24 cm): orange
- Chenille wire, 6$\frac{1}{2}$" (16 cm): blue
- Chenille wire, 6$\frac{1}{2}$" (16 cm): pink
- Chenille wire, 6$\frac{1}{2}$" (16 cm): light green
- Chenille wire, 2$\frac{3}{4}$" (7 cm): silver
- 2 half-pierced untreated wooden beads, about 1$\frac{1}{8}$" (3 cm) in diameter
- Silk flower, about $\frac{3}{4}$" (2 cm) wide
- 4 cotton balls, about $\frac{1}{2}$" (1 cm) wide
- 10 cotton balls, about $\frac{3}{4}$" (2 cm) wide
- Poster board: white
- Adhesive-backed pads, $\frac{1}{2}$" (1 cm) thick: white
- Template

> **Tip**
>
> Use as a regular picture frame to display photos and postcards, or use as a door sign or mirror frame in a child's room.

At Home with the Monsters—Frame or Mirror Decoration

Cut white paint with an equal amount of water and apply a wash to the picture frame. Paint the monsters as shown. For the blue monster, make the eyes and nose from painted paper and attach with masking tape or glue pads. To make the hair for the pink monster, cut the blue aluminum wire into five pieces and wind them around a pencil to make spirals. Attach at the back of the bowl with hot glue. Attach the silk flower to one spiral.

To make the hair of the blue monster, cut the silver wire into four pieces and attach the painted cotton balls to the ends. Glue them and the silver chenille wire at the back of the bowl. Make the hands from painted wooden or cotton balls and attach to the chenille wire ends. Glue the wire to the back of the handle.

Add distance between the spoons and the frame with adhesive-backed pads. Glue the arms of the pink monster to the frame and tie on a piece of checkered ribbon. Bend the arms of the blue monster into shape.

Colorful Acrobats Mobile

Following the template, drill three holes into the spoon. Paint the spoon, spatula, and hollow string as shown in the picture at left. Paint on the patterns with a toothpick. For each hairpiece, fold the raffia to the length desired and tie the ends in knots. Attach to the back of the spatula with hot glue.

Cut four toothpicks into three pieces each. With hot glue, attach one end of each to a painted cotton craft ball and the other end to the hollow string. Attach the rubber tubing to the back of the spatulas at the base of the acrobats' heads. Bend the chenille wire pieces into shape and secure to the back of the hands with hot glue. Tie on a length of yarn.

Thread a painted wooden bead onto each piece of yarn, then thread string through the hole in the bowl and secure with a knot. Thread the central string through both spoons. To keep the spoons in a cross shape, attach the cotton craft balls as shown. Cut two 12" (30 cm) pieces of yarn, thread through the outermost holes in the spoons, and tie in a knot. Hook both pieces on the first spiral of the metal spring.

Materials for Colorful Acrobats Mobile

- 2 wooden spoons, round bowls, about 2" x 12³/₄" (5 x 32 cm)
- 5 raclette spatulas, 5¹/₄" (13 cm) long
- Matte acrylic paint: beige, pink, apricot, orange, moss, lemon yellow, kelly green, sky blue, bright pink, yellow
- Poster board: white
- 12 cotton craft balls, about ¹/₂" (1.5 cm) in diameter: white
- 5 moss rubber hollow tubes, about ¹/₄" (8 mm) in diameter, 4" (10 cm) long: white
- 1 chenille wire, 9¹/₂" (24 cm): white
- Raffia, 28" (70 cm) long: orange, emerald green, bright pink, light blue, yellow
- 5 pierced untreated wooden beads, about ¹/₂" (1.5 cm) in diameter
- Yarn: white
- 1 metal spring, about ¹/₂" x 8" (1.5 x 20 cm)
- Template

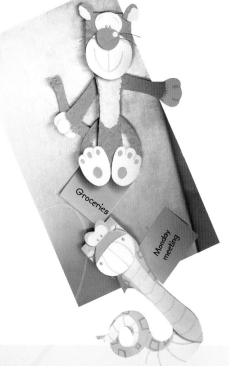

The Elephant and His Friends

Elephant

Paint all pieces as shown. Attach the paper pieces with masking tape. For a 3-D effect, underlay the trunk with adhesive-backed foam pads. Attach the painted sisal wire just below the bowl with hot glue and attach a wooden bead to each wire end. Attach the spatula to the handle with hot glue. Decorate the notepad with poster board and glue it on as well. Attach the test tube and rubber mount. Bend the arms around the spatula.

Widen the hole of the tree stand, if necessary, to match the diameter of the handle. Put the half-bead on the handle. Insert the handle in the tree stand and glue the half-bead to the base.

Snake and Leopard

Make the snake's eyes, nose, tongue, and tail, as well as the leopard's eyes, muzzle, limbs, ears, and tail, from poster board. Paint all the pieces and the spatulas, and add the patterns with a toothpick. To make the leopard's whiskers, glue $1/2$" (1.5 cm) pieces of binding wire behind the nose. Bend the wire into shape. Attach the eyes and ears of the leopard with masking tape. Attach the noses of both animals with foam pads. Attach the limbs and tails at the back and attach the leopard's feet at the front with foam pads. Attach two magnets at the back of each figure.

Materials for Elephant

- 1 wooden spoon, round bowl, about $2^1/8$" x $12^3/4$" (5.5 x 32 cm)
- 1 raclette spatula, $5^1/4$" (13 cm) long
- Matte acrylic paint: ice blue, sky blue, lemon yellow, apricot, pink, honeydew melon
- Poster board: white
- Sisal wire, about $1/2$" (1 cm) thick, $8^3/4$" (22 cm) long
- 2 wooden untreated wooden half-beads, about 1" (2.5 cm) in diameter
- 1 pierced untreated wooden bead, about $1^1/8$" (3 cm) in diameter
- Adhesive-backed foam pads: light blue
- Notepad
- Test tube, 5" (12.5 cm) long
- Rubber test tube mount
- 1 tree stand, $1/2$" x $2^3/4$" x $3^1/2$" (1.5 x 7 x 9 cm)

Materials for Snake

- 1 raclette spatula, $5^1/2$" (13 cm) long
- Matte acrylic paint: lemon yellow, pink, sky blue, light blue, bright green
- Poster board: white
- 2 magnets, about $3/4$" (2 cm) in diameter

Materials for Leopard

- 1 raclette spatula, $5^1/4$" (13 cm) long
- Matte acrylic paint: pink, apricot, light blue, sky blue
- Poster board: white
- Binding wire, about $1/16$" (0.5 mm) in diameter, $2^1/2$" (6 cm) long: orange
- 2 magnets, about $3/4$" (2 cm) in diameter
- Template

Materials for Frederic Fox Bulletin Board and Timetable Holder

- 1 wooden spoon, round bowl, about 2$\frac{1}{8}$" x 12$\frac{1}{8}$" (5.5 x 30.5 cm)
- 3 untreated wooden half-beads, about 1" (2.5 cm) in diameter
- 1 pierced untreated wooden half-bead, about 1$\frac{1}{8}$" (3 cm) in diameter
- 1 crafting stick, 5$\frac{3}{4}$" (14.5 cm) long
- Poster board: white
- 2 pompoms, about 1$\frac{1}{8}$" (3 cm) in diameter: white
- 1 pompom, about $\frac{3}{4}$" (2 cm) in diameter: pink
- Embroidery floss, 2" (5 cm) long: white
- Matte acrylic paint: orange-brown, dark brown, turquoise, light turquoise, salmon, lemon yellow
- 1 cork coaster, about 5$\frac{1}{2}$" (14 cm) in diameter
- 1 tree stand, $\frac{1}{2}$" x 2$\frac{3}{4}$" x 3$\frac{1}{2}$" (1.5 x 7 x 9 cm)
- Template

Frederic Fox Bulletin Board and Timetable Holder

Make the wooden and paper pieces as shown. With masking tape, attach the ears at the back and the hat at the front of the bowl. Thread the pink pompom onto the yarn, tie the end in a knot, and attach to make the bobble hat.

To make the arms, attach the wooden stick to the back of the handle. With hot glue, attach a pompom to each end, and on top of that glue the wooden half-beads. Attach the cork coaster to the handle with hot glue.

If necessary, widen the holes of the half-bead and the tree stand to match the diameter of the handle. Put the half-bead onto the handle, attach the handle to the tree stand, and glue the half-bead to the base.

109

Materials for Fun Farm Clothes Rail

- 3 wooden spoons, oval bowls, 2" x 13^1/$_2$" (5 x 34 cm)
- Matte acrylic paint: beige, dark brown, salmon, honeydew melon, bright green, ice blue, light blue, apricot, pink
- Antique varnish
- Balsa wood, ^{1}/$_8$" (4 mm) thick
- Small metal bell, about ^{1}/$_2$" (1.5 cm) in diameter: gold
- Raffia: natural, light yellow
- 1 plastic daisy, about ^{1}/$_2$" (1.5 cm) in diameter
- Aluminum wire, about ^{1}/$_{16}$" (1 mm) in diameter: white
- Chenille wire: apricot
- Poster board: white
- 4 pieces of sisal wire, about ^{1}/$_2$" (1 cm) thick, 7" (18 cm) long
- 2 pieces of sisal wire, about ^{1}/$_2$" (1 cm) in diameter, 5^1/$_2$" (14 cm) long
- 8 wooden feet, 1^1/$_8$" x 1^1/$_2$" (3 x 4 cm)
- 4 wooden feet, 1" x 1^1/$_2$" (2.5 x 3.5 cm)
- 2 rubber hollow tubes, about ^{1}/$_4$" (7 mm) in diameter, 1^1/$_2$" (3.5 cm) long
- 2 pierced untreated wooden half-beads, about 1^1/$_2$" (3.5 cm) in diameter
- 1 shelf with wood brackets, with additional board at the back, about ^{1}/$_2$" x 6" x 18" (1.5 x 15 x 60 cm)
- Screws
- Dowel
- 3 wooden knobs, about 1^1/$_8$" (3 cm) in diameter
- Template

Fun Farm Clothes Rack and Shelf

Shorten two spoons to 7" (18 cm) in length (cow, horse) and one to 5¼" (13 cm) in length (pig). Varnish the longer spoons, let dry, and then paint the cow white, leaving the varnish exposed in some places to create the cow pattern. Paint the bowl of the pig pink and the handle sky blue.

Paint the cow's eyes. Attach the raffia and tongue to the back of the balsa-wood muzzle, and then glue it onto the bowl. Paint the horse's eyes. Attach the wired flower at the back of the muzzle before attaching it to the face. Make the mane with 1⅛" (3 cm) raffia.

Attach all ears directly to the edge of the bowls. Do the same with the cow's horns and the pig's snout. Shape the pieces to the curve of the bowl if necessary.

Attach the painted sisal wire at the back of the bowl to make the limbs and glue the wooden feet to all ends. Attach a wooden half-bead to the cow and horse handles. Tie on the cowbell with raffia and secure it with glue. Attach the tails to all the animals: for the cow and horse, use painted hollow rubber tubing with glued-in raffia tassel; for the pig, use chenille wire.

Mix paint with an equal amount of water and color-wash the shelf. Paint the knobs with regular paint. To assemble the shelf, attach the brackets to the upper board about 1¾" (4 cm) from the side and then screw on the other board from the back.

Attach the front hooves of the cow and horse to the top board. To attach the pig, drill the board two-thirds in the diameter of the handle. Attach the handle with wood glue. Put up the shelf with frame hangers or with screws and dowels.

Materials for Baby Gnome Pacifier Holder

- 1 wooden spoon, round bowl, about 2" x 12³/4" (5.3 x 32 cm)
- Matte acrylic paint: beige, light blue, apricot, light orange, lemon yellow, pink
- Poster board: white
- 2 cotton craft balls, about 1" (2.5 cm) in diameter: white
- Raffia
- 2 small metal bells, about ¹/2" (1.5 cm) in diameter: gold
- 1 small metal bell, about ³/4" (2 cm) in diameter: gold
- Sisal wire, about ¹/2" (1 cm) in diameter, 12" (30 cm) long;
- 1 pompom, about ¹/2" (1 cm) in diameter: light blue
- 4 pompoms, about ¹/2" (1 cm) in diameter: white
- Template

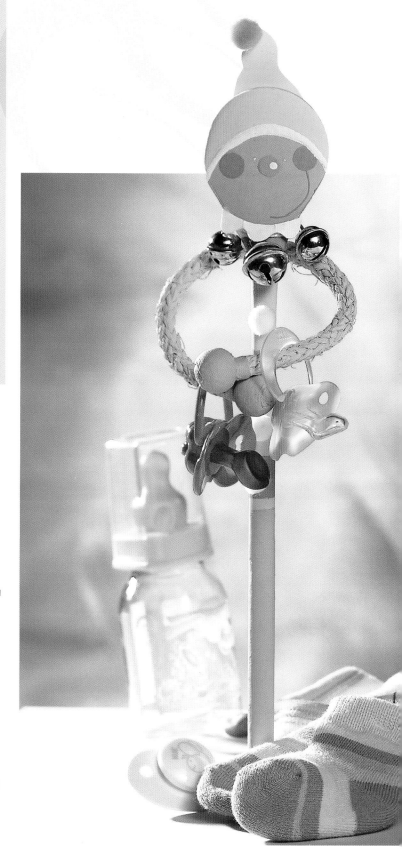

Baby Gnome Pacifier Holder

Paint the spoon as shown. Make the hat and collar from paper. Glue the pompom to the hat and attach all pieces. Thread the bells onto the raffia, make a knot after each one, and tie around the neck. Decorate the spoon with pompoms.

Center the sisal wire to the back of the handle and glue in place. Cover the wire ends with masking tape to keep them from fraying. To make the hands, carefully widen the holes of the cotton craft balls with small scissors, and attach the wire ends with hot glue. Paint the cotton craft balls and any masking tape that still shows.

Nibbling Kitty Goody Jar

With a coping saw, cut the spoon to match the height of the jar. Paint the spoon and paper parts as shown. Paint the fine lines with a toothpick. Attach the back paws with foam pads to the bottom of the bowl. Attach the front paws to the bowl with masking tape. Bend up the left front leg slightly and decorate with a hard candy. Attach the chenille wire tail to the back of the bowl.

Decorate the jar with curly ribbon: cut fifteen pieces of ribbon, each 4" (10 cm) long, splice in the middle, and attach all around the jar with masking tape. Cover with a piece of corrugated cardboard; to give the edge a wavy pattern, cut it with craft scissors. Attach the handle to the back of the jar with hot glue.

Materials for Nibbling Kitty Goody Jar

- 1 wooden spoon, round bowl, about 2" x 14" (5 x 35 cm)
- Matte acrylic paint: orange, pink, light blue, bright pink, ice blue
- Poster board: white
- Chenille wire: white
- Corrugated cardboard, about 1.6" (4 cm)- wide strip that is the length of the jar circumference: green
- Crafting scissors with wavy pattern
- Curly ribbon, about 5' (1.5 m): light green
- 1 glass jar with screw-on lid, about 4" (10 cm) in diameter, 7" (18 cm) high
- Template

Materials for Beppo the Clown Pen Holder

- 1 wooden spoon, round bowl, about 2" x 12$^3/_4$" (5 x 32 cm)
- Matte acrylic paint: beige, light blue, red, sky blue, emerald green, salmon, yellow, orange
- Poster board: white, light blue
- 3 pompoms, about $^1/_2$" (1 cm) in diameter: white
- 1 pompom, about $^1/_2$" (1 cm) in diameter: red
- Crafting wood, 5" (13 cm) long
- Raffia, about 17$^3/_4$" (45 cm): white
- Curly ribbon, about 8" (20 cm) long: shiny orange
- 1 washcloth, about 5" x 6$^1/_2$" (12.5 x 16.5 cm): red
- Washcloth, felt, or fabric scraps: light blue, orange
- Iron-on fleece scrap
- 2 wooden buttons, about $^3/_4$" (2 cm)
- 1 tree stand, $^1/_2$" x 2$^3/_4$" x 3$^1/_2$" (1.5 x 7 x 9 cm)
- Iron
- Thread
- Template

Tip

The small pocket on the front of the trousers can be used for erasers, paper clips, stamps, and so on.

Beppo the Clown Pen Holder

Paint the clown, craft stick, and tree stand with acrylic paint. Make the bow tie, hat, and hands from poster board. Make the patterns with acrylic paint. Glue the pompom to the hat. Make the dots on the bow tie and tree stand with a cotton swab. Add new paint after each dot for an even pattern.

Glue the craft stick to the back of the handle and the hat to the front of the bowl. Attach tightly curled ribbon pieces, about 2" (5 cm) long, to the back of the bowl. Attach the pompom nose with hot glue.

To make the trousers about 4$^3/_4$" (12 cm) long, fold over the bottom end of the flannel and secure the fold with a few stitches at the back. Cut a hole in the center of the fold (to put the wooden handle through later). Make the hole smaller than the diameter of the handle to make sure small utensils do not fall through.

To make the suspenders and the small pocket, iron fleece to the back of the fabric to keep it from fraying. (Leave the top rim of the pocket exposed, as it will be folded over.) Be sure to follow the manufacturer's instructions for the iron-on fleece carefully. Cut the pocket and suspenders (as shown on the template sheet) and sew onto the trousers. Add buttons to the suspenders and sew on the pompoms. To gather the trouser opening slightly, use a needle to thread raffia through the upper rim of the trousers. Pull the trousers over the handle and place the suspenders over the craft stick. Finish by attaching the hands and bow tie with masking tape.

Materials for 3-D Ocean Scene

- 2 wooden spoons, round bowls, about 1³/₄" x 8" (4.7 x 20 cm)
- 1 wooden spoon, oval bowl, 1³/₄" x 12" (4.8 x 30 cm)
- 1 wooden spoon with pointed tip, 2" x 12" (5.2 x 29.5 cm)
- 1 collector frame, 3¹/₈" x 8¹/₈" x 12¹/₈" (8 x 20.5 x 30.5 cm)
- Poster board: white, light orange, gold, red
- Corrugated cardboard scrap: pink
- Cardboard, 8¹/₂" x 11" (about A4)
- Metal foil scrap or tinsel: pink, bright pink
- Matte acrylic paint: yellow, gold, light blue, lemon yellow, bright green, pink, sunshine yellow, lilac, ice blue, bright pink, sky blue
- Glitter paint: turquoise
- Shells
- Template

3-D Ocean Scene

Shorten the wooden spoon for the shark to 6" (15 cm) (cut at a slight angle); for the jellyfish, 6³/₄" (17 cm); for the fish, 4³/₄" (12 cm); and for the submarine, 10³/₄" (27 cm). Paint all wooden and paper parts, as well as the cardboard for the background, in the colors shown. To make the gradient color for the fish, paint the top part of the bowl lemon yellow and the bottom part bright green, and mix the colors together in the middle with a cotton swab. Add the fine lines with a fine brush or toothpick. Make the dots evenly with a cotton swab. Apply a light blue base coat of paint to the handle and the background cardboard. Add the sky blue waves and decorate them with glitter paint.

Attach the poster board pieces to the front and back of the bowl with masking tape. Add the foil strips in two colors for the jellyfish, glue them to the bowl, and then cover the join with a strip of corrugated cardboard, ¹/₄" x 3" (7 mm x 8 cm).

Paint the frame white and glue on the painted background cardboard. Attach the animals in a staggered 3-D pattern to the frame with hot glue or wood glue and stabilize with a thin nail if necessary. Glue on the water plants and shell.

Cut the red poster board to match the frame, cut out the patterns, and glue to the frame.

Mary the Bug Hanging Rail

Paint the spoon as shown. Make the nose from poster board and attach with an adhesive pad. Bend the aluminum wire as shown and attach the painted cotton craft balls to two pieces. Attach all wire pieces at the back of the bowl with hot glue. Start the holes for the hooks with a needle, spacing them evenly. Screw in the hooks, using pliers if necessary.

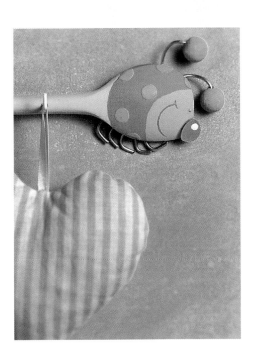

Tip

Hang small, lightweight objects like keys, hair accessories, or a sachet on the rail.

Materials for Mary the Bug Hanging Rail

- 1 wooden spoon with pointy tip, $1^3/4$" x 12" (4.5 x 30 cm)
- Matte acrylic paint: light pink, pink, lemon yellow, kelly green, light blue
- 7 aluminum wires, about $1/16$" (2 mm) in diameter, $1^1/8$" (3 cm) long: silver
- 2 cotton craft balls, about $1/2$" (1.5 cm) in diameter: white
- Poster board: white
- 5 screw-in hooks, $3/4$" (2 cm) in diameter: white
- Template

Mad Bird Plant Decorations

Paint the spoons as shown. Apply a base coat first, let dry, and then paint with brushes of various sizes. Add details with toothpicks. Cut out the balsa wood pieces and paint them. Dab on the dots with a cotton swab, applying new paint after each dot for an even pattern.

For the green bird, dab hot glue onto the three white wire pieces and insert them in the balsa-wood pieces. Attach the other end of the wires at the back to the bowl. For the red bird, curl the wire and attach at the back of the bowl.

Attach the feathers at the back of the bowl with glue. Attach the wings at a slight angle. For the red bird, attach the feet to the chenille wire and then glue this to the back of the bowl. For the green bird, glue the feet to the front of the bowl.

Materials for Mad Bird Plant Decoration

- 1 wooden spoon, round bowl, about 2" x 12³/₄"–14¹/₄" (5 x 32–36 cm)
- Aluminum wire, about 0.04" (1 mm) in diameter: white
- Balsa wood, ¹/₈" (3 mm) thick
- Matte acrylic paint: black, bright green, orange, apricot, sky blue, red, light blue, lemon yellow or bright pink
- Marabou feathers: turquoise or lilac
- Chenille wire, 4" (10 cm) long: orange
- Template

Spoon Buddies for Spring

Finally, the gray days of winter are over and spring is near. Now, new wooden spoon projects are awaiting you, in the shape of cheerful decorations for indoors and out, and some useful little helpers for various tasks. Get your wooden spoons out of the kitchen drawer and start with these fun projects. How about an attractive napkin holder chicken or an inviting door sign? See for yourself—wooden spoons look good anywhere and everywhere!

– Monika Gänsler
Contributing Author

Tender Spring Welcome

Paint the handle of the wooden spoon spring green and the body peach and slate blue. Drill the holes. Draw the face and glue on the cheeks. To make the hair, wind wire around the raffia and glue it to the head. Cut out the wings from Mikado paper and attach to the back. Glue on the head, decorate the inscribed heart with two small flowers, and attach it to the handle.

Thread the cotton wool cord from the back through the hole, add a beige wooden bead to each side, and secure with a knot. Finish by putting the butterfly into the peach-colored tree stand; secure it with glue and decorate the case with small flowers.

Materials for Tender Spring Welcome

- 1 wooden spoon, oval bowl, 12" (30 cm) long
- Poster board scraps: pink, beige
- Mikado paper: light blue, pink
- Matte acrylic paint: spring green, peach, slate blue, beige
- 2 wooden beads, about $1/2$" (12 mm) in diameter, with about $1/8$" (3 mm) hole
- Raffia: light green
- Cotton wool cord, about $1/16$" (1 mm) in diameter, 6" (15 cm) long: natural
- 5 flowers, about $3/4$" (2 cm) in diameter: pastel colors
- 1 tree stand, $1/2$" x $2 3/4$" x $3 1/2$" (1.5 x 7 x 9 cm): natural finish
- Template

Flower and Bee Hanging Rail

Drill the holes, insert the rounded wooden skewers and secure with glue. Paint the spoon spring green, the untreated wooden half-bead medium yellow, and the wooden beads olive green. Attach the wooden beads to the skewer pieces with glue.

Shade the petals with a yellow pencil, assemble the poster board flower, and glue it to the spoon. Place the painted half-bead in the middle of the flower.

Glue the strips and the heads to the bees' bodies cut from poster board. Attach one wing each to the front and one each at the back. Glue the bees to the wooden handle with hot glue. Attach the finished rail with glue pads.

Tip

This rail can be used for all the little things gardeners like to have close at hand.

Materials for the Flower and Bee Hanging Rail

- 1 wooden spoon, round bowl, 12³/₄" (32 cm) long
- Poster board scraps: dark green, white, sun yellow, beige, dark brown
- Matte acrylic paint: spring green, medium yellow, olive green
- 1 rounded wooden skewer, about ¹/₁₆" (3 mm) in diameter, 4³/₄" (12 cm) long
- 3 wooden beads, about 1/2" (12 mm) in diameter, with about ¹/₁₆" (3 mm) holes
- 1 untreated wooden half-bead, about ¹/₂" (15 mm) in diameter
- Yarn: black
- Template

Snapdragon

1440 annuals

Small Snail Stick

Paint the handle peach and decorate with light blue dots. Paint the bowl peach with apple green dots and add a light blue and light pink stripe.

Glue the eyes and the pompom nose to the poster board snail, draw all the lines, and color the cheeks with a red pencil. Make the antennae from thick binding wire and attach at the back. Attach the snail to the front with a hot glue gun.

Double the ribbon, wind thin binding wire around the top, thread the wire ends through the buttonholes, twist them together, and curl the ends. Attach the bow to the handle just below the snail.

Materials for Small Snail Sticker

- 1 wooden spoon with pointed tip, 12" (30 cm) long
- Poster board scraps; white, light green
- Matte acrylic paint: light blue, apple green, peach, light pink
- 1 pompom, about $1/4$" (7 mm) in diameter: black
- 1 button, about $1/4$" (6 mm) in diameter: light blue
- Ribbon, 2" x $17^3/4$" (5 x 45 cm): light blue
- Template

Materials for Pansies Flower Forever

- 1 wooden spoon, round bowl, $12^3/4$" (32 cm) long
- 1 wooden spoon, round bowl, 10" (25 cm) long
- Felt scraps: olive green, white, orange, yellow, dark blue, light blue
- Matte acrylic paint: beige, scarlet, spring green
- 2 untreated wooden half-beads, about $1/2$" (15 mm) in diameter
- 1 rose pot, about $3^1/2$" (9 cm) in diameter
- 1 rose pot, about $2^3/4$" (7 cm) in diameter
- Ribbon, 1" x 48" (2.5 x 120 cm): yellow
- Raffia: natural
- Dry floral foam
- Coconut fiber: green
- Template

Pansies Flower Forever

Paint the handle spring green and the bowl beige. Draw the face, add the scarlet nose, and attach the felt petals and leaves at the back. Fill the clay pots with dry floral foam, tie raffia around them, and attach the raffia with binding wire and some glue. Insert the pansies into the foam, secure them with all-purpose glue, and tie the bows around their necks. Finish by covering the foam with coconut fiber.

Materials for Flower Peg for Garden Gloves and Small Garden Tools

- 1 wooden spoon, oval bowl, 10³/₄" to 12" (27 to 30 cm)
- Felt scraps: dark green, white
- Matte acrylic paint: medium yellow, spring green, olive green
- 1 dowel, about ¹/₁₆" (3 mm) in diameter, 1¹/₂" (4 cm) long
- 1 wooden bead, about ¹/₂" (12 mm) in diameter, with about ¹/₁₆" (3 mm) hole
- 2 decorative ladybugs, ¹/₂" (1.5 cm) long
- Template

Flower Peg for Garden Gloves and Small Garden Tools

Drill the hole for the crafting stick into the handle. Glue the stick into the hole. Paint the handle spring green and the bowl medium yellow. Glue on the olive green wooden bead, felt petals and leaves, and lady bug. Paint small black dots on the middle of the flower. Attach to the wall with a frame hanger or glue pad.

This Way to the Garden

Paint the bowl beige, the handle spring green, and the area for the shoes ultramarine blue. Drill the holes and draw the face. Attach the front pocket to the cape and push it from the bottom onto the handle. Attach the wooden beads and paint them beige. Make the beard from angel wool; apply glue to the appropriate area and then push the wool against it. Cut the beard into the desired shape with scissors. Glue together the felt hat. Add the hat and nose to the figure.

Secure the gnome in the spring green–colored tree stand with hot glue. Glue on the shoes and decorate the bucket with the daisies. Be sure the hot glue gun isn't too hot!

Assemble the strawberry, inscribe it, and hang it from the arm with yarn. Put a flower in the front pocket and attach the cape to the arms with a bit of glue.

Tip

If your oval spoon is a little long, simply cut it to size. Alternatively, leave it as is and make the decoration a bit bigger

Materials for This Way to the Garden

- 1 wooden spoon, oval bowl, 10³/₄" to 12" (27–30 cm)
- Felt scraps: blue, red, yellow, olive green
- Poster board scraps: red, green
- Matte acrylic paint: beige, scarlet, ultramarine blue, spring green
- 1 tree stand, ¹/₂" x 2³/₄" x 3¹/₂" (1.5 x 7 x 9 cm): natural finish
- 1 untreated wooden half-bead, about ¹/₂" (15 mm) in diameter
- Angel wool: white
- Yarn: green
- 1 zinc bucket, about 1¹/₂" x 1³/₄" (4 x 4.5 cm)
- About 12 daisies
- 2 wooden beads, about ¹/₂" (12 mm) in diameter, with about ¹/₈" (3 mm) hole
- 1 dowel, about ¹/₈" (3 mm) in diameter, 5¹/₂" (14 cm) long
- Template

Cheeky Ladybug for Candy

Paint the spoon beige, then paint the forehead black. Drill the hole into the handle. Draw the face and glue on the poster board nose. Attach the pompoms to the antennae and glue these to the back.

Make the felt piece according to the template sheet and put it on the handle from the bottom. Insert the chenille wire in the drilled hole below the cape.

Attach the lady bug to the vessel with a hot glue gun. Put the chenille wire ends through the handles and thread the wooden beads onto the wire. Attach to the vessel.

Decorate an ivy leaf with a small ladybug. Glue this leaf and one more to the vessel. Finally, tie the bow around the neck of the ladybug.

Materials for Cheeky Ladybug for Candy

- 1 wooden spoon, round bowl, $12^3/4$" (32 cm) long
- Felt, 7" x 7" (18 x 18 cm): red
- Poster board scrap: red
- Matte acrylic paint: black, beige, carmine red
- 26 pompoms, about $1/4$" (7 mm) in diameter: black
- Chenille wire, $16^3/4$" (42 cm) long: black
- 2 wooden beads, about $1/2$" (15 mm) in diameter, with about $1/4$" (4 mm) hole
- Ribbon, 1" x 18" (2.5 x 60 cm): dark blue
- Decorative ladybugs, $1/2$" (1.5 cm) wide
- 2 decorative ivy leaves, about 3" (8 cm) long
- 1 zinc vessel, about $4^3/4$" x $8^1/2$" (12 x 21 cm)
- Template

Materials for Springtime

- 1 wooden spoon, round bowl, 12³/₄" (32 cm) long
- Poster board scraps: red, golden yellow, dark green
- Matte acrylic paint: spring green, peach, scarlet, slate blue, orange
- Wooden letters, 1¹/₂" (4 cm) high
- Twigs
- Feathers: orange
- Template

Springtime

Paint the handle peach and the bowl spring green. Assemble the poster board head, draw all lines, and attach the feathers to the back of the head. Glue on the head and both wings and feet. Draw the feathers on the body. Tie thin binding wire around a small bunch of twigs. Paint the wooden letters in different colors and attach them to the handle.

Happy Easter! For the Easter Bunny and His Helpers

Paint the spatula spring green and inscribe. Assemble and paint the poster board rabbit, attach it to the top of the spoon, and add the poster board Easter eggs. Paint the Easter eggs in light pink and ice blue. Fold a piece of raffia, wind binding wire around it, curl the ends, and glue to each egg. Decorate the brush with the eggs. Wind binding wire around some hay, curl the ends of the wire, and glue to the spatula.

Materials for Happy Easter

- 1 wooden spatula, 11½" (29 cm)
- Poster board scraps: dark brown, blue, yellow, light blue, lilac
- Matte acrylic paint: spring green, light pink, ice blue
- Hay
- 2 cotton wool eggs, ¾" (17 mm) high
- Raffia: natural
- Template

Baa-Lamb

Paint the handle spring green and the bowl ivory. Drill all holes. Wind the ribbon in a spiral patterns around the handle. Attach one end of the ribbon to the back of the handle with glue. Wind the ribbon around the handle and attach the other end at the back of the handle.

Attach the feet to the wire legs, let dry, and then insert one wire in each hole and glue to secure. Attach the metal bell to the body with thin binding wire and curl the wire ends. Color the nose and cheeks with a red pencil and then attach the assembled head. Finally, tie a bow on the handle.

Materials for Baa-Lamb
- 1 wooden spoon with pointed tip, 10" (25 cm) long
- Poster board scraps: ivory, beige, dark brown
- Matte acrylic paint: ivory, spring green
- Satin ribbon, 1/4" (6 mm) x 11" (28 cm): light green
- Satin ribbon, 1/4" (6 mm) x 12" (30 cm): light green
- Brass bell, about 3/8" (9 mm) in diameter
- Template

135

Materials for Lamb Place Cards for the Easter Table

- 2 raclette spatulas, 5¼" (13 cm) long
- Poster board scraps: beige, ivory, dark brown
- Matte acrylic paint: spring green
- 4 decorative daisies, about ¾" (2 cm) in diameter
- 2 bells, ½" (1 cm) high
- Hay
- Template

Lamb Place Cards for the Easter Table

Paint the spatula for each sign spring green. Assemble the head and glue to the body. Make two holes in the body with a hole punch, write the names, and attach the bell with thin binding wire. Scratch the indicated fold with a needle and attach body to the spatula.

Wind thin binding wire around the hay, curl the wire ends, and glue it onto the spatula. Add the daisies.

Bon Appétit! Funny Napkin Holders

Duck

Paint the spatula olive green and white and make the holes. Assemble the head, draw all lines, and add the feathers. Then add the wings and head. To make the legs, thread the cotton wool cord through the holes, thread on the orange wooden beads, and secure them with a knot. Paint the clothespin olive green, inscribe it, and add the peg to the bottom.

Materials for Bon Appétit! Funny Napkin Holders

- 2 raclette spatulas, $5\frac{1}{4}$" (13 cm) long
- Poster board scraps: white, red, sun yellow
- Matte acrylic paint: orange, spring green, olive green
- 4 wooden beads, about $\frac{1}{2}$" (12 mm) in diameter, with about $\frac{1}{8}$" (3 mm) holes
- Cotton wool cord, about $\frac{1}{16}$" (1 mm) in diameter, 12" (30 cm): natural
- Feathers: white
- 2 wooden clothespins, 3" (7.5 cm) long: natural finish
- Template

Chicken

Make the chicken as described above, except add the comb and neck only; do not add feathers. Paint the clothespin and the handle of the raclette spoon spring green. Shade the cheek dot with a red pencil.

Songbird

Paint the handle spring green and the bowl indigo blue. Assemble the head and draw all lines. Glue the wire curl to the back of the bowl and attach the head to the body. Glue the blue feather to the back, the white one to the front. Make a bow from the ribbon, glue a ladybug on it, and attach the bow to the handle. Glue another ladybug to the handle.

Materials for Songbird

- 1 wooden spoon with pointed tip, 10" (25 cm) long
- Poster board scraps: white, red, golden yellow, dark blue
- Matte acrylic paint: indigo blue, spring green
- Feather: white
- Feather: blue
- Ribbon, 1" x 32" (5 x 80 cm): light blue
- 2 decorative ladybugs, $1/2$" (1.5 cm) long
- Template

Flower Child for the Beginning of Spring

Paint the spoon beige, spring green, and light blue. Draw the face and paint the wooden beads beige. Glue on the raffia hair, then add the felt bell hat. Thread the cotton wool cord through the hole, thread on the wooden beads, and secure them with knots. Make the hole with a hole punch, tie on a satin ribbon, and drape the cape around the handle. Attach the spoon to the tree stand with hot glue gun, glue on the coconut fiber, and add the inscribed poster board sign.

Materials Flower Child for the Beginning of Spring

- 1 wooden spoon, round bowl, 8" (20 cm) long
- Poster board scrap: ivory
- Felt scraps: dark blue, dark green
- Matte acrylic paint: beige, light pink, spring green, light blue
- Satin ribbon, $1/8$" (3 mm) x 12" (30 cm): green
- 2 wooden beads, about $1/2$" (15 mm) in diameter, with about $1/8$" (4 mm) holes
- 1 tree stand, $1/2$" x $2^3/4$" x $3^1/2$" (1.5 x 7 x 9 cm): natural finish
- Raffia: light green
- Coconut fiber: green
- Cotton wool cord, about $1/16$" (2 mm) in diameter, 7" (18 cm) long: natural
- Template

Big Chick Easter Nest

Drill the holes into the handle and insert the wooden stick. Paint the handle and the stick spring green and the bowl white. Paint the wooden bead olive green and attach it to the stick. Assemble the poster board chicken, draw all lines, and glue it to the spoon. Attach both legs and add the last lines. Hang the conical basket on the hook. Attach the nest to the wall with a frame hanger or glue pads.

Tip

You can find large spoons like this in kitchen stores. If you can't find the precise size, simply adapt the template to suit a smaller spoon.

Materials for Big Chick Easter Nest

- 1 wooden spoon, round bowl, about 3³/₄" x 13¹/₂" (9.5 x 34 cm)
- Poster board scraps: red, white, light brown, golden yellow
- Matte acrylic paint: spring green, olive green
- 1 rounded wooden craft stick, about ¹/₈" (4 mm) x 2¹/₈" (5.5 cm)
- 1 conical wicker basket, 13¹/₈" (33 cm) long
- 1 wooden bead, about ¹/₂" (15 mm) in diameter, with about ¹/₈" (4 mm) hole
- Template

Materials for Easter Bunny Thermometer

- 1 wooden spoon, oval bowl, 10" (25 cm) long
- Felt scrap: dark brown
- Matte acrylic paint: beige, scarlet, olive green
- Cotton wool cord, about $1/16$" (2 mm) in diameter, 7" (18 cm) long: brown
- 1 untreated wooden half-bead, about $1/2$" (15 mm) in diameter
- 1 wooden indoor thermometer, 6" (15 cm) long
- 1 tree stand, $1/2$" x $2^3/4$" x $3^1/2$" (1.5 x 7 x 9 cm): natural finish
- Patchwork fabric strip, $1^1/8$" x 10" (3 x 25 cm)
- Template

Easter Bunny Thermometer

Paint the spoon beige, the tree stand olive green, and the half-bead scarlet. Drill all holes. Complete the face. Thread binding wire from the back through both holes and curl the ends. Attach the nose and add the raffia hair. Thread the cotton wool cord through the hole and glue on the felt paws. Attach the ears at the back. Insert the spoon in the tree stand, secure it with glue, and add the hind paws. Glue on the thermometer and attach the front paws. Tie on a strip of fabric as a scarf.

Easter Tree for the Easter Table

Paint the handle spring green and the bowl white. Drill all the holes into the handle and the tip of the spoon. Insert the sticks and glue into place if necessary. Glue a wooden bead to each end. Paint the sticks and the beads indigo blue and peach.

Attach a satin ribbon to the back of the handle top, wind it around the handle in a spiral pattern, and glue it to the back of the bottom of the handle. Attach both feathers and the assembled head. Glue the feet behind the feather tips.

Insert the spoon in the olive green tree stand and secure with hot glue. Decorate the tree stand with coconut fiber. Paint the cotton wool eggs in pastel shades, attach a piece of raffia to each egg, and hang from the tree.

Materials for Easter Tree for the Easter Table
- 1 wooden spoon with pointed tip, 12" (30 cm) long
- Poster board scraps: red, white, golden yellow
- Matte acrylic paint: spring green, pigeon blue, peach, scarlet, olive green
- 1 dowel, about 1/8" (4 mm) in diameter, 4³/4" (12 cm) long
- 1 dowel, about 1/8" (4 mm) in diameter, 6¹/2" (16 cm) long
- 1 tree stand, 1/2" x 2³/4" x 3¹/2" (1.5 x 7 x 9 cm): natural finish
- Satin ribbon, 1/4" x 14" (0.6 x 35 cm): light blue
- 2 feathers: white
- 5 cotton wool eggs, 1¹/8" (30 mm) high
- Raffia: natural
- Coconut fiber: green
- Template

Planting Tags for a Hobby Gardener

Paint the handles spring green and the bowls orange or carmine red. Draw the eyes and all lines. Glue on the leaves and stems. Glue on the painted clothespins and attach the inscribed signs.

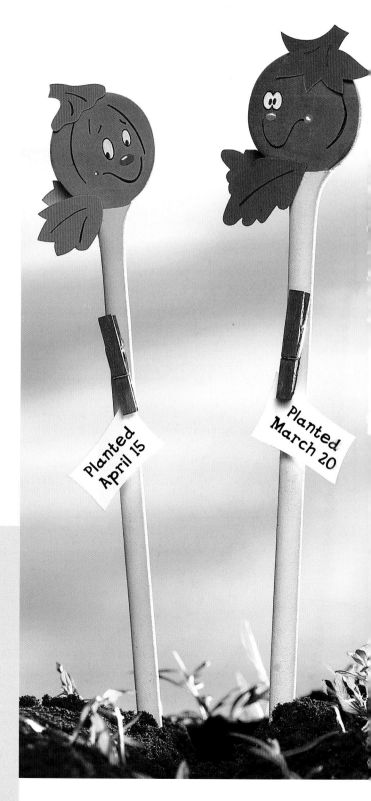

Planted April 15

Planted March 20

Materials for Planting Tags for a Hobby Gardener

- 2 wooden spoons, round bowls, 12³/₄" (32 cm) long
- Poster board scraps: dark green, white
- Matte acrylic paint: carmine red, orange, fir green, spring green
- 2 wooden pegs, 1³/₄" (4.5 cm) long
- Template